CW00431705

SOMEWHERE TO GROW
The story of a garden

by

Jane Whittle

THANKS to my daughter Gael Henry for the drawings, to my
granddaughter Naomi Cahen for the design, to all the family who
helped with the book and to many friends who helped to look after
the garden over the years, particularly Agnes, Andrea and Bev.

Ty'r Gawen 1996

Jane Whittle
SOMEWHERE TO GROW The story of a garden

© 2012, Jane Whittle
Self publishing
jane.tyrgawen@googlemail.com

ISBN-13: 978-1475131970

All rights reserved. No part of this publication may be reproduced,
stored in retrieval systems or transmitted in any form or by any
means, electronic, mechanical, photocopying, recording or otherwise
without prior written permission of the copyright owner.

This book is dedicated
to David and our
children, the garden
was created for theirs.

CONTENTS

INTRODUCTION

'I have returned to earth
completed many journeys, now
is the time to make a garden in
a wilder place.'

The best reason for writing a book is because you
have something to say. When I came to live in
Wales I thought that more time and space would provoke more words. The opposite happened. I began to
feel that there were too many books, too many words
already, and that I had nothing to add to them. Instead,
I began to make a garden.

On Easter day three years later, my son, on a visit from
London with his family, said, 'Why don't you write about
this?' The valley was sparkling in warm spring sunshine,
the garden was full of daffodils; the cat was rolling on
the primroses; the children were watching ducklings being taught to dive on the pond. 'You never showed us
how to make a garden'.

That did it. The seed was planted; it would grow, and
it might be fruitful. A grandmother's garden became

'Somewhere to Grow'. The world is changing so quickly all kinds of things are being forgotten. When I was ten my father showed me how to put up fence posts, but I never showed my children how to do it. Many things which I took for granted because they were part of everyday life when I was a child, they have had to learn from books, or have not learned. I grew up able to recognize almost all the common birds in the British Isles; somehow my children did not, probably because they spent their earliest years in a city. The green revolution is something that is happening to city bred people; those brought up in the countryside before or during the second world war did not need to be told how to make compost or keep chickens, but much of what was common knowledge then has been forgotten, or ignored, since. I doubt if anyone, fifty years ago, would have dreamed of feeding chickens their own entrails.

We all want to pass on what has been useful to us, even if it may often seem there is no longer a useful place for it. I believe passionately that we must maintain our connection with the natural world in meaningful ways or we will destroy ourselves, each other and the place which supports us. We are not in charge of it, but we have tremendous responsibilities. We are part of a miraculously complex, continuously creative cosmos, and to neglect our connection is perilous. Although all this is being acknowledged at last, it is not yet being practiced. Not so long ago it was generally supposed that mankind would eventually learn to master everything, although there have always been some cultures that have known better.

Gardening, growing things, is no longer a necessity for most of us, but has become a very popular pass time. Garden centres, garden visiting, gardening on television,

garden magazines and books all reflect the needs, perhaps, of an over urbanised society. We look for ways to
balance the situation when choices are limited; as soon
as we were released from continuous manual labour we
began to fill our spare time with other kinds of physical activities, many of which were once essential for
survival – like fishing, sailing, running and walking – or
gardening.

The third age, often called retirement, is a wonderful
opportunity to live more independently. Time, as they
say, is your own; you do not have to spend so much of
it doing what someone else expects or wants you to do.
You have a choice. If you are lucky enough to have some
space as well as time, the world is your oyster and you
have a chance of creating a pearl, whatever it might be.
It could be a garden.

Of course, you do not have to be retired to make a
garden. If you are, you may be a bit short on muscle
and money, but you have the most important ingredi-
ent – time. If you are younger you may be stronger but
unsure how to make the best use of less time. I am in the
first category and shall be describing how I do it now, by
myself, without hiring a digger or a planner and spending almost nothing. I also have my children in mind, and
theirs, so I shall explain some of the tricks I have learned,
hoping they may be useful – how to recycle everything
and avoid expenditure; how to minimize physical effort;
how to enjoy the more repetitive tasks; how to make best
use of the weather, the site and its existing features; how
to fit in with the miraculous processes of life and create
something which I hope will be 'a joy for ever'.

I shall tell the story of how it happened to me, and
perhaps why. I may dig up unexpected things, strange

seeds may germinate which I did not know had been planted. That is the way of it, for writing and gardening, Everything is part of this creative process of growth and change and, if we try too hard to control it, we may waste energy, or block it. When we co-operate, miracles begin to happen. It is my experiences of all this that I hope to pass on, now that I have hung up my boots, returned to earth and put down roots.

I am not an expert. My garden is something I work with and learn from – a continuing event I help to happen. The weather and location have a lot to do with it, as do people who encourage me or give me plants and those who come and enjoy it. Gardeners grow things in different ways. Some spend a lifetime producing prize-winning giant vegetables or perfect blooms that only last a day. Others plan, hire a JCB, plant it all in a year and then do as little as possible for ten. A garden is a personal creation. You can draw with light and shade, paint with flowers and sky, make sculpture with earth, rocks, trees, old iron or cement; enjoy the sounds of water and birds, the scents of blossom and the movement of the wind. For me a garden may also turn into poetry because I cannot help trying to put things into words. The gardens I like best offer both spaces to explore and places in which to be, places to sit and empty oneself of all the cares of the world and let go. Nothing pleases me more than when other people find peace and pleasure in my garden too. I hope the story of this garden will inspire new gardeners, and old ones too.

Diary entry:

May – As I write a small black duck waddles by,

pecking at the night scented stock that has just come into flower under the honeysuckle where I sit. The smells are intoxicating. As I look out across the valley the view of oak woods, sheep meadow and distant sea is framed by ceanothus, a cutting from my son's London garden which his wife gave me three years ago. Now it is five feet tall, its elegant branches laden with blue flowers, arching over blue hills, somehow resisting the prevailing wind. Below are the yellow spikes of flag iris collected from the wild and, nestling under a rock beside the pond, the yellow polyanthus which has bloomed continuously, with their feet in the water, since Christmas. A small weeping willow, also a cutting, bends over them, its feathery fronds waving across the shade behind. Lambs bleat, ducklings take off across the pond like tiny paddle steamers and the cat comes to sit on my papers. 6 o'clock – time to feed the animals.

Chapter 1
MAY

Of MIRACLES, metaphors, shaping land and finding water...

> 'I hate quotations.
> Tell me what you
> know...'

Emerson. Journals 1849.

My garden is in Wales, a country where rural life is still intimately involved with seasonal time and influenced by the shape and structure of the land. The Celts, and the people who lived here before them, were closely involved with animals, growing things and the places which sustained them – springs, lakes and rivers; hills, rocks and trees; the weather and the seasons; the movements of tides, sun, moon and stars and their effects upon the earth. Farmers and gardeners everywhere have always had to attend to these things, but scientific knowledge and technical innovation have made them

feel less dependent on them. Now that I am physically
closer to them myself I am able to live a life that is influenced more by the dictates of the natural world than
by the necessities of nine to five and the goading of the
media.

The Celts celebrated the beginning of summer, as we
do, in May, at the festival of Beltaine, the time of greatest growth. They counted time in nights rather than days
and the beginning of the Celtic year was at the winter
solstice, when the days grow longer again but there is
still time to dream new dreams during the long hours of
darkness. We rarely give ourselves such time, but, for me,
a night walk marked such a beginning. Seeds germinate
in the dark, but what better time to open a garden diary than the time when the garden is most alive and the
gardener most hopeful, the active season of sowing and
growing which starts, in Wales, on May Day.

> *Midnight – May 1st.*
> *I have been walking in the garden. The full moon*
> *is reflected in the pond so brightly it seems to jump*
> *out of the water towards me, much brighter than the*
> *moon floating in the sky above. Reflections are like*
> *that – as dreams can sometimes seem – more real*
> *than what provoked them. I can stand with one moon*
> *at my feet and another above my head, as if the light*
> *were travelling through me and, when the night breeze*
> *gently moves the water and the bright moon quivers,*
> *I feel a shock like pins and needles, in muscles, bones*
> *and blood.*
> *This is not the first time a potent May moon has*
> *offered inspiration. I slept beneath one once, during*
> *a night of full eclipse, and conceived a book about*

journeys into the distant past made on foot. This time, being a little older, I hoped I would not need to stay out all night, or walk so far. But I was seeking similar stimulus.

The silver birch rustles its leaves and I remember how I carried it in my pocket from the New Forest. Now, as it shivers and sways, each new leaf catches the light and they all twinkle like stars. The stone walls, the paving, the rocks, trees and water, all look more dramatic by moonlight. Imperfections, and compromises do not show up in this light. The lawn is soft underfoot, I cannot see the weeds. The air still smells of honeysuckle, broom and stocks. It seems incredible that a few years ago none of this was here. Beyond the garden, lights twinkle along the edge of the sea three miles away. The huge, shadowy hills stretch up into the night sky and one light shines out from across the valley. I wonder if they can see my light too.

I want to share all this and yet I revel in my private presence in it. Is it an illusion? It is a kind of magic, a perfection, this patch of paradise? I am a little frightened that the spell might break. William Blake wrote, 'He who clasps to himself a joy, does it's winged life destroy'. I have always remembered those lines. My mother read them to me when I was young enough not to question them. Is the process of writing about and trying to communicate something so illusive a kind of clasping? We have to move on and let the moment go, as children do. There is no end to the procession of present moments.

When we look back over the years, remembering, we

sometimes come across patterns in events which were imperceptible when they occurred. They only make sense later. I discovered that a garden, as a metaphor, had featured in poems that puzzled me when I wrote them. In retrospect I can see that they may have been cathartic in the way that dreams can be. Now they appear to be milestones from an inner journey which took me from a childhood garden, out into the world, half way round it to the Himalayas, then round and round again on maze-like journeys exploring my own country on foot, then, eventually, to this garden – ' to the place I started from'. My earliest memory is of running happily down a steep path between tall daffodils until someone shouted, 'Slowly – be careful!' I can still feel the sense of puzzled frustration that caused. Travelling alone is one way of taking charge of your life and finding out about yourself and others. Today many young people are able to travel, but I was middle aged before I managed it. Years later, returning from trekking in Ladakh and visiting Buddhist monasteries, I wrote a garden poem which ended –

> '... retracing outward paths,
> returning home from other lands,
> I find her waiting
> in the place she started from
> among tall flowers.
> The magic must begin at home.'

But it was several more years and journeys before I understood what I had written. Travelling on foot through Nepal and Ladakh were life changing experiences which eventually led me back to explore ancient tracks in Britain. Now I realise I had to travel outward, and inwards, to re-discover the simple knowledge of here and now that children have. We all get tipped out of the first garden to set out alone. The journey is symbolized by the maze which returns us to the beginning, the spiral path of the pilgrim. That is how it works – coming to accept what is, what we are and where. Then we can operate more freely from our own creative space, with patience and trust.

Inspiration, the breathing in of an idea from an empty space, comes first; then comes the form, the shape it will take and what goes into it – whatever it is, is going to be – a cake, a book, a poem, a painting or a garden. A good way to look at the shape of a garden is to walk about in it by moonlight. I discovered that moonlight simplifies by emphasizing light and dark – the intricate edge of a fern or the sheen of a camelia leaf. That night the lawn gleamed like a polished table, the water like a silver dish laid upon it; plants were massed together in mysterious shadow or leaped out as individual dancers, delicate and graceful, caught in a spotlight.

Perhaps the most important thing about a garden is its shape. Without shapes to define them colours loose their power. Light and shade creates structure. One small, bright flower catching the sun can sing out against a dark background, whereas it could look insignificant somewhere else. The contrasting shapes of single leaves, or trees and their shadows, can be just as exciting as colour. Shapes are also made by walls, paths, pergolas and arches, as well as by planting. The third dimension is all important. Even in the smallest garden you can create perspective – a view from, into or through things, upwards as well as sideways.

The first thing I did was to look at what was already there. Then I considered what I would like to add to it, bit by bit. One thing leads to another. If you inherit something you do not like it is a matter of deciding what to get rid of. I was lucky to have a place with a good basic shape and all kinds of natural assets, like a fabulous view and running water, and nobody had spoiled it. A solid stone farmhouse, with yard and barns, set in a south facing hollow in the hillside, overlooks the valley, with mountains to the south and east and, to the west, the sea. The hollow is the quarry which provided most of the material for the buildings. The site slopes downhill, with a spring at the top and a small stream that flows through the plot and out into the ditch at the edge of the meadow. There is very little soil at the back, which is not well drained, so it suits bog plants like iris, peppermint and willow. The bank at the top is dry and windswept, but heather grows well there, as do cistus, hydrangea and Azalea. In front of the house there is a little clay, good for natural ponds, and the stone buildings protect it all from frost. There is a small orchard, overhung by huge ash trees in a wood which shelters the site from the north. Mountains provide shelter from the killer north east wind, but the warm west wind surging in from the sea can batter things to bits.

When I first saw it there was a small lawn in the front, surrounded by six foot high Japanese knotweed, fearsome plants which behave like trifids. There was a row of beans, a lot of nettles and ground elder sheltered by a hedge of wild plum, hazel and thorn. Periwinkles were scrambling all over the stone walls of three pig sties and ivy was interlaced with the roof slates. The rest of this half acre was very rough, rank grass. In the boggy bits brambles had climbed twenty feet into elder and holly trees and rushes and buttercups were choking the stream.

As soon as I saw it, I loved it. Immediately I thought of things I could do. On that first cold, dark November day of wind and rain, there was water everywhere; standing in puddles, spurting out of mole holes, splashing from drain pipes and gurgling in the stream. Water was to be the first element I worked with. It was like a return to childhood, when every holidays my brother and I would make a new den or divert a stream.

It was Maytime when I returned as owner of this little patch of land and its stone buildings. I was hardly able to believe my luck. A lot of water had flowed under the bridge but my dream had come true, in the end. The strange thing was that I had, in fact, only just abandoned a lifetime's longing to live in such a place and decided that, if I could never manage it myself, I could always visit people who had. And then it happened. I believe now that things often work out like that; as if you have to let go of needs and wants and let things take place in their own way. But you do have an objective in mind so you are ready to go for it when an opportunity arrives.

As I walked towards the back door on that momentous day and stepped into the slate flagged hall, sunlight was streaming in through the windows and swallows were swooping round the eaves. I know I had come home at last. I walked the boundary and sat for a while by the spring. The water was bubbling out of a dark hole hidden by ferns and foxgloves. I decided to begin by cleaning out the stream. It was so choked with vegetation water had been flooding the yard and coming in under the door. I ripped out great blankets of grass from the surrounding rock with the aid of an invaluable tool

my daughter had found in the Portobello Road market.
It was a first World War trenching tool – designed to be
attached to the barrel of a rifle. Without this magnificent
implement the garden might have defeated me. It has a
short, well balanced wooden handle with a robust steel
pick/shovel on the end. I use it for weeding, planting,
digging, hacking and earth moving. It is best used sitting
down, which avoids overuse of the fragile and aging
lower back. With this tool weeds and rushes came out of
the gravel bed of the stream quite willingly. I cut back
undergrowth like hair, with sheep sheering clippers I
bought in a car boot sale for 10p. My father had some
smaller ones which he always used for cutting lavender.
By the end of that first day a clear, dancing stream was
flowing all the way down from the spring to the boundary ditch. Then I decided to divert it and make a small
waterfall near the back door where, one day, we would
sit and listen to its soothing sound on summer evenings.

Water has helped to shape the garden. After that first
eventful day of symbolic activity – helping the water to
flow again – I began to discover how the site had been
drained originally.

There is one deep land drain which carries water from
the french drain at the back of the house into the ditch.
During a weekend visit the previous November I had
followed the winding course of water bubbling up out
of bog until I unearthed an old stone chamber three feet
down which could once have been a well. Once this was
rodded, and the three other land drains which crossed
the yard into an ancient stone manhole, the water level
dropped by about eight inches. In an old house it is advisable to hunt out these old drains before spending a
fortune on damp courses. My son, digging in the bog,

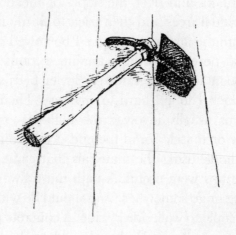

also discovered a leak in the main water pipe about two feet down which could have been there for years. No wonder there were so many rushes.

The stream itself runs in a rock hewn channel to one side of the house and through the pig sties to the field ditch. I began to plan the diversion and the waterfall before I moved in. I drew endless sketches on winter evenings, reading a little book on Zen gardening which shows you how to arrange rocks and water so they look like mountains and lakes in miniature; how to mystify and intrigue; how to please and pacify. I sketched the real mountains and river, the slopes of meadow, woods and individual trees and then tried to fit my imaginary garden into the larger landscape. I borrowed gardening books and pored over the planning sections but most of them contained diagrams of flower beds seen from above, which I found hard to envisage. Their building instructions usually involved too high an expenditure of money or muscle so, in the end, I had to invent my own methods, using the materials that came to hand. But some tips were useful. A path must always lead to something or go somewhere and should be wide enough for two people to walk side by side. A concrete path from the back door already lead to the old earth closet, now mysterious under ivy, and on through the veg' patch to the orchard. I used cinders and builders rubble for two more, to the compost heap and the bonfire. I laid plastic under old slates and small stones for paths between the veg' plots and cut a few paths through the long grass behind the house. Once the main routes through the garden had been established useful shapes emerged.

Meanwhile I was planting cuttings and small trees all over the place, trying to imagine how things might

eventually develop. I would stand and squint at diminu-
tive saplings leaning out of their new holes and walk
round them, stepping back, looking at them from windows and seats or doorways to envisage how the full
grown tree might frame the view, cast a shadow or hide
a telegraph pole. Now that they are beginning to look
like real trees I can see that sometimes I got it right, but
not always. Some have already been removed; a few
shrubs are already too big, but at least they have grown
and survived the gales. I needed to find out what would
thrive, and where. At first I did not think I would be able
to grow roses because of the winds from the sea, but, I'm
glad to say, I was wrong. Four year later the barn wall is
covered with kiftsgate and maigold, madam alfred car-
riere is a mass of fragrant white blooms on the windy
front of the house, New Dawn prolific pink in the shade
at the back. I can hardly wait for the albas, which thrive
in boggy jungle, to flower for the first time next month.

Planning is continuous as things grow and shapes
change, but I soon discovered that the structure of this
garden was already there. An old leat, which was supposed to bring water to the mill next door, became a
high path through the quarry, along which I gradually
planted seedling trees – hazel, may, ash, birch and holly,
with bluebells and blue hydrangeas which do well in a
woodland setting. As the trees grew there was less rank
grass to cut and brambles began to give way to ivy. The
old farm track just below had been cut from the rock
and these cliffs and banks provide a solid structure which
simply needed emphasis. I made a bridge out of slab of
slate from the pig stye floor where the track crossed the
stream, and put a seat nearby – a few solid boards on
blocks. This suggested another pond under a heap of

boulders where I planted lilies and primulas which love the damp and dappled shade. My brother gave me a selection of willow cuttings – they quickly took over the edge of the stream. Then I made some rough steps from the track up to the leat path where rock roses did well on the dry bank and ramblers and honeysuckle clambered up to meet the blackberries.

Bit by bit I dug out brambles and stripped blankets of couch grass from the rock. Once exposed it contrasted well with un-mown grass. Rock does not need mowing, it soon grew moss and lichen instead. Piled up weeds turned into useful compost and stripped turf could be used to level grassy areas or build up a bank. I began to learn about finding, storing a re-using all kinds of materials. There was a huge heap of builders' rubble in the yard. It was full of stone, lime plaster and bricks. The bricks were used to make steps and paths and the stone to edge the ponds. The remains of the pile drained well and for the first few years was a riot of nasturtiums. Now it is the most trouble free part of the garden. When I look out of the bathroom window I see an arching dog rose, the silver leaves of Senecia, which is a mass of yellow in summer and white stars of periwinkles which scramble through everything and flower all the year round. Their shiny dark green leaves contrast well with the lime green euphorbia, a thicket of purple sage and a self seeded crop of daisies shooting orange sparks at it in July when the greens are beginning to get out of hand. The elegant shrub called Leycesteria, with its droopy blood red flowers, moved in on its own and nasturtiums still peep out here and there. A purple hebe and a red berried cotoneaster complete a self-sufficient jungle of colour which settled down well against the grey stone walls of the barn behind, with its rambling roses, sprouting ferns and pennywort.

May is such a beautiful month I avoid doing anything which denies me a moment of it. I put off shopping until I run out of animal food, feeding myself on eggs and broccoli. Once the seeds are in, the grass has been cut and before the weeds overtake me, there is time to sort out all the old bits of iron that appear wherever I dig – anything from a horse shoe to an iron door hinge. We found an 18th century butter churning wheel three feet across buried outside the dairy. It had once been turned by a horse. I stack old bricks, make piles of useful stones, and pick up shattered slates, old bottles and broken china from the chicken run, which must have been a rubbish heap for hundreds of years. I write out of doors and read in the hammock strung between the old apple trees. One day the pine and the birch, the first two trees I planted on the front lawn, will be big enough to sling a hammock closer to the house. I invite people round to enjoy the garden with me and relax by the stream in the evening with a glass of elderflower wine. At this time of year the goats, with their three young billies, first took up sunbathing. Flowers are coming into bloom so fast I want to slow everything down.

May.

After weeks of sunshine, it has rained. Even the air is green. Now I understand why, in Tibet, green is the symbolic colour of air – in a dry land air is greener than earth. A heavy shower does more good than hundreds of watering cans. You only have to spend a month or so in a dry land to appreciate the miracle of rain, and begin to wonder why we waste so much of it. Everything is suddenly greener. The trees breathe out a green haze and the smell of moisture meeting dry soil is intoxicating. The honeysuckle makes me sneeze. The trees fill out; first those golden oaks across the valley, then the tall ash in the wood – that means a good summer. Bluebells appear between the glowing gorse – all the land changes colour and everything looks so sleek and hopeful. But all too soon the daffodils are over, the petals from the clematis float like snowflakes on the wind from the sea, new shoots bend and break. The grass is growing too quickly and up come the weeds. The magic of Maytime, that urgent sense of wonder and hope, moves into summer, with long, light evenings and the fragrance of roses.

Chapter 2
JUNE

Of TIME, smell, doing and being and the Summer Solstice.

'Because I know that time is always time
And place is always place
And what is actual is actual for only one time
And only one place
I rejoice that things are as they are...'

T.S. Eliot

This is the time of year to spend hours gazing at your garden. Occasionally it is too hot to work, but, even if it isn't, as soon as the sun comes out and the mowing has been done, the best thing to do is pour a long cool drink and sit down somewhere. This is summer and may not last long. I have half a dozen different kinds of seats, so I try them all in turn, enjoying the view from each and considering what might be done to improve it. In July and August there will be visitors and no time to ponder.

In June, in good weather, every garden looks wonderful and there is more daylight. Unlike plants, office workers have electric light to keep them going in winter. Growing things can be produced that way, and are, but they do not taste so good. Extending the active time artificially may not be so good for people either – seasons and phases of the moon affect us too. Perhaps office and school hours should be varied according to the time of year as farm work used to be. At this time of year everything is shooting up towards the sun and nights seem very short pauses in the process. Sometimes I wake up and think I can hear things growing.

June.

All this month, in spite of sudden downpours and occasional gales which batter the roses and flatten the hay, everything grows and blooms. The flower beds are a riot of colour. I keep on weeding and cutting grass; I sit and gaze; I walk about visiting plants and make notes about changes I want to make. The red currant and the broom, both burning bushes in spring, have grown too big and will need pruning – the first by removing old branches in winter, the second by clipping now, but not into the wood. Several colour combinations need sorting out. Some things have been submerged and need rescuing. The giant lupin has been killed by a plague of greenfly – the only pest problem since the ducks dealt with slugs and snails. The horrible mixture I made with nettles in a water butt is ready for pouring onto the tomatoes and courgettes. I make elderflower wine, cordial, champagne and fritters. I wander around in the evening, watering the new roses, comparing their scents and counting my blessings.

The first rose to come out is maigold, on the barn wall.
I have planted Golden Showers, another tough one, with
a vigorous rambler, Bobbie James, to follow. Madam
Alfred covers the pergola and flowers almost continuously throughout the summer, resisting gales well. Then
comes etoile de hollande, a rich crimson beauty with a
scent that knocks you over, with old fashioned pink May
Day which I bought for the name. Compassion climbs
through the vine by the kitchen door and the tough albas
are taking over the bog. The pretty pink Fairy and Bal-
lerina flower in the borders for months on end if I dead
head them; New Dawn climbs over the front door and
albertine, which I grew from a cutting, produces gorgeous salmon coloured buds along the front wall. Blush
noisette and felicite et perpetué scramble over arches
and up trees – a profusion of cool pink and white pet
als like whipped cream. Kiftsgate, which covered fifteen
yards of wall in three years, is a stunning sight later on
and the pig sties will one day display the huge single yellow flowers of the slow growing Mermaid, which I first
saw growing on a very special barn in east Anglia. The
cutting I took from that rose now climbs to the top of
a silver birch in a Wiltshire garden and this one is its
progeny. The most recent addition are Paul's Himalayan
Musk to twine with honeysuckle and overrun the boundary fence, and several elegant David Austin English roses
to grace the flower beds around the lawn – Heritage, St
Cecilia, Sherifa Asma, L.D.Braithwaite and Sweet Julie.
Dapple Dawn, which I planted too near the gate, was
attacked by sheep, and had to be moved.

roses are the glory of the summer garden – dreamed
of during winter evening poring over romantic names
and glamorous pictures in catalogues. I like to see them

growing rather wild, as ground cover and scrambling over trees. The choices are endless, from original species roses to the modern developments which incorporate most of the best qualities of their ancestors, something to suit every setting. In June smell creates another dimension. Pausing to smell a rose as you go by is a feature of a maturing garden; you build up those pleasurable habits if you put fragrant things close to where you sit or walk. I have a standard Iceberg where I can greet it without bending down and it looks wonderful against the blue distance of the mountain seen from the kitchen. I found four of them on a garden centre rubbish heap after dreaming of a row of them in front of the house. Two lived for a year but only this one survived for three. After they died I built the pergola instead. Smell is so important I wonder if any rose without a smell is worth the money.

I love the exotic, Mediterranean smell of sticky cistus; it always brings back memories of my grandmother. Even in summer she dressed in sweeping long skirts of Donegal tweed, with tweed knickers underneath; she wore heavy gold rings set with opals and garnets on her boney fingers and wound string around them to prevent them falling off. I can see her now, with her *pince nez* on her nose and a shady hat, sitting in her cliff top garden among the cistus, gazing out to sea. Smell seems to provoke memories more than any other sense; I wonder if my love of roses has anything to do with the fact that, as a very small child, I was put out in my pram for a summer afternoon nap in my father's rose garden. It is good to plant memories.

All our senses can be stimulated in a garden. Sight we take for granted, as long as we have it, but sometimes we may not notice the sounds made by birds, water or wind. But silence is precious too and, in some gardens, difficult to come by. A thick hedge is the best protection from the noise and smell of a busy road; a fence covered with climbing plants may be better than a wall because it absorbs vibration. A waterfall can mask unwelcome sounds from elsewhere. Plant the most fragrant things where you sit and walk. Roses and honeysuckle over the cottage door were no accident. What is more refreshing than coming in to tea after a long day outdoors through a fragrant porch like that, especially after rain. And these joys repeat themselves year after year.

Retirement, or the third ages, releases us from many notions of time, yet some people find this too strange and immediately re-invent a timetable with deadlines. This seems a pity when here is a chance to experience life in a different kind of way, like the cat who goes hunting one day and then curls up by the fire the next, depending on the weather or inclination. Time, if it really exists, is a very flexible commodity. We cut it up into fixed, predictable units. Maybe this was what our forbears were doing when they built Stonehenge – inventing time. We have turned it into a jealous God. We try to 'make the best use' of it to 'get things done'. 'Things' become enemies that assail us until we imprison them by crossing them off the list. I have been like this most of my life so I know it is not the best way to enjoy what you are doing.

That triumphant egg-laying feeling of having completed everything on the list only lasts a minute because the new list is already forming. The stressful build up lasts much longer than the relief of having nothing left to do. There are those who are actually scared of having nothing to do. I am not one of those. Nowadays I try to write down only those things that could be disastrous if I forget them. Most things, like the squeaky door will remind me of themselves eventually. This does not mean I have stopped doing things; I am doing them more selectively with less fuss and increased enjoyment. Future events need not become a worry in advance.

Ideas are born from the spaces between things, so it is necessary to create gaps – in both time and space. As we grow older, we need more rest days to brew up energy and, like the stream, thoughts flow more clearly when the weeds have been cleared out. There are those days when energy is low, after a late night or a long drive. Then it is silly to attempt to hack turf from rock or dig the vegetable patch. A mood of martyrdom is a sure way to physical damage or accidents. On such a day I would be well advised to sit in the sun on the bank with the trenching tool and gently extract buttercups and couch grass from the heather, taking plenty of rests to gaze out across the valley towards the bright line of the sea and listen to the cuckoo calling from the oak woods. On Aldous Huxley's 'Island' there were Minah birds trained to call out 'Here and Now!' all the time, to encourage everyone to live in the present moment.

All gardeners know that there are good and bad times for doing things. The state of the soil dictates activities. Weeds come out more easily after rain, but they may grow again if left lying there; in dry weather they will die with their roots in the air. Digging is easier when the soil is not heavy and sticky with moisture; grass is impossible to cut when it's wet ; earth moving can be quite easy when the soil is dry. The idea that you must finish one job before you start the next, which I was taught at school, makes no sense in the garden. I learned this

from an old gardener, watching him lean on his spade
and dream, while a robin collected worms within inches
of his boots. He would tie up roses when his back was
aching from digging; sweep leaves after hoeing; attend
to things in the greenhouse sitting on a stool during a
shower of rain. Everything is going on at once anyway
so if one job gets too boring or exhausting there is always another waiting to be done. Then there are the
more subtle timings to do with weather or the moon. It
is better to plant things when the moon is waxing but
it is better still if you do it on a day when you feel like
helping something to grow, when you are not in a hurry,
not in the ten minutes between mowing the lawn and
getting the supper. I have found that the times when I
feel like sowing seeds or planting things are often at the
right stage of the moon anyway. Similarly pruning is
safer when the sap is not rising.

If you do something when you feel like doing it you
will probably do it better. If you do it only because you
think you ought to, resentment can get in the way. Of
course money is a good motivator, but a better one is
someone who appreciates what you do. To do it because
you love it is best of all.

In a world torn by horror and hopelessness and con-
trolled more and more by competition, it may seem
rather useless to spend time and energy making a garden. However, if it gives you joy it will give others joy
as well, and the more people who try to live a life that is
creative and kind, the better. As I grow older I am more
impressed by extraordinary 'ordinary' private people
than I am by public figures. What we learn from the media is never quite true; what we experience is. Perhaps
thoughts are like pebbles thrown in a pool, they may

have a knock on effect and spread further than we realise. There is a professor of engineering in America who
has been working experimentally for years on the small
effects people's thoughts can have on the behaviour of
electronic machines – I am sure I upset my computer!
Would our grandparents have believed that we could sit
in our arm chairs and see what was going on in India?
There is so much we still don't know. Once the small
miracles begin to happen, which they do if you let them,
bigger ones may. I know people who worry about their
garden and I understand their feeling because I used to
be one of them. I remember calling a friend, who was a
budding horticultural journalist, to ask her advice about
weeds. I showed her my problem, which was really too
much land and not enough time, and she was appalled.
'I don't know what to suggest, ' she confessed, having
based her experience on a few tubs and square meters
of earth, 'maybe you need some help'. She was right.
I was brought up to garden but always overestimated
what I could manage. Gardening became a chore, like
housework. So I did not do it very well and it did not
repay my efforts. I became a slash and burn gardener,
struggling with a lawn mower that would not start, chest
high nettles, buttercups, ground elder and couch grass.
But even then, I could not imagine life without a garden.

You have to be honest with yourself. There are only
two reasons for gardening – one is to produce tasty,
seasonal food that will do everyone more good than
anything you can buy; the other is for pleasure, which
includes the pleasure of picking, eating and storing your
own fruit and vegetables. If you do it to impress people
it would be easier to dress well or make a success of another job. Unless it is also your profession, a garden is

only for enjoyment. Otherwise, fill a few containers with plants from the market, lay a few slabs for the barbecue and cover the rest with an old carpet until you feel differently about it.

These days it is trendy to order gardens from experts in the same way as you order a new kitchen or car, as an amenity. It comes complete and almost maintenance free; a few years later you get a new one. You have little to do with it except that you have to earn the money to buy it. You use it as an outdoor extension to your home and for summer entertaining. But it doesn't matter what other people do. If you like rhubarb you could grow nothing else. Or plant asparagus or apple trees or all the year round radishes. Or swing a hammock and surround it with things that smell good. Or let it all grow and see what happens. I visited a permaculture garden once and asked what they were growing in the poly tunnel. 'Oh,' was the gentle reply, 'we are waiting to see what comes up'. You are in charge of your garden, as far as anyone is in charge of anything in the natural world. You put your time and energy into it; nature puts hers. The combination can be many things, depending how much time you have. She has a lot more. Plan your garden to contain your dreams, but not to run away with them.

Time is on your side. If you don't get it right the first season, something else will happen next.

One year all my young vegetables were eaten by slugs and snails. I had built so many stone walls for them to breed in that, when I walked across the lawn at night, I crunched armies of them marching towards the lettuces. I bought a pair of ducks and two years later the vegetables were thriving, there were more ducks and a lot less snails When the ducks ate the watercress I had to move it. One summer I left the geese to eat the grass and then wondered why there were no gooseberries. So I made fences and small gates out of old roofing battens and sheep netting; they keep the geese out of the garden and prevent visiting dogs from chasing the ducks. They help to protect the lettuces from rabbits and the potatoes from badgers.

Much has changed since my parents were gardening. Fewer people grow vegetables; more people travel and a garden can be a tie. We all look for labour saving solutions. The traditional large, and very productive, country house garden relied on paid labour, which few of us have any more, but a totally labour saving garden can be a bit boring. I enjoy the more natural overgrown effects and try to combine the single handed, frugal cottage garden approach – marigolds among the cabbages, self sown poppies and aquilegia, roses round the door – with the gracious, spacious generosity of a country house where everyone comes to relax. The difficulty is scale; the landscape is huge, but I can only lift small boulders. I hope this results in some kind of unity. These days, unlike those times when I first had my own garden, I am not in a hurry. Tomorrow is another day and, in June they are long ones. A little bit at a time is the secret of gardening in the third age. 'Slowly, slowly', as the Sherpas say to tourists puffing up their mountains.

June 21st   Mid-summer Solstice.
   I woke at four this morning. I can never sleep through the shortest night. Mist from the river lay across the valley right up to the garden. The pool was a precious stone, an opal or moonstone, shining at the edge of a luminous white veil. Distant trees floating

*above it seemed to move closer; hedges and woods be-
came part of the garden. The sycamore tree outside
the gate was a massive, dark shape against the pale
blue bulk of the hills, leaning towards the house. The
hills too seemed to float closer on this shifting sea and
the standing stone stood out starkly above the track
where it disappeared into the cloud. As I watched,
the mist began to slip away down the meadow like a
blanket, as if the earth were rising out of it, turning
over into the longest day, taking a deep breath and
letting the night covers slide gently away across the
green pasture, down to the wood, through the hedge
and over the road, revealing bit by bit the small details
of trees and fences, until it was swallowed by shining
loops of river. I had been privy to an early morning
process of waking and changing, a re-arrangement
of light and shade. I felt as if I had been let into
a secret. Then a cock crowed, the northern sky grew
pink as I dressed and walked out into this mysterious
early morning world of birdsong, cobwebs and dew.
A water rat arrowed its way across the mill pond; a
blackbird burst into song in the hedge; geese and goats
were surprised to see someone at this private hour and,
as I reached the crest of the hill, I interrupted cows
feeding their calves, dark, motionless shapes against a
red dawn sky.*

*I had hoped to see the moon go down as the sun
came up but the mist was rising again. I watched
the last star in the east climb over the electricity wires
and marvelled at its speed of movement, of the earth
turning. Seagulls flew overhead and their wings were
tinged with pink, but the mountain was sinking into
the rising mist. Would the sun come up before the*

mountain disappeared? I think the sun and cloud ar-
rived together. Only the sea gulls saw the sun rise; as
I turned to go their wings had turned to gold. The col-
ours changed again. The meadow is no longer green,
but silver, gold and pink; as a breeze moves the hay
it shines like flowing water. The jackdaws start their
noisy day and I can hear the roar of the waterfall in
the next valley.

* * *

Now it is dusk, the end of the longest day, my fa-
vourite hour According to the Tibetan system this is
the best time for people with a fiery nature; we rest
when the sun goes down and the best place for us is in
the west. Two Irish grandfathers may be responsible
for my inclination towards the mists and mysteries of
the sunset shore. The Tibetan theory certainly fits the
inhabitants and history of Celtic lands. This is the
'happy hour'. The birds strike up conversations again
after snoozing through the heat of the day; I have
fed the chickens, the ducks, the geese, the goats and
the cat. My supper is in the oven; I have laboured
enough for one day, so I fill a tumbler full of elder-
flower wine and orange juice and take it to the seat
below the ponds. From there I look back at the house
through a frame of white roses which are softening the
outline of grey stone. I am enclosed by flowers. This is
a sitting spot which has only recently been 'mystified'
by a new flower bed designed to hide it from the house.
I have planted roses, clematis and sweet peas to climb
over the arch above the seat. A delicate fuchsia leans
out from the low stone wall beside me, flanked by some

strange insect like lavender. An almost black pansy is peeping from some self sown forget-me-knots. Because I wanted forget-me-knots at my wedding, my mother clipped them back all through May on June – we were married on Mid-summer day. I can smell the orange blossom just behind me and looking at the house from here gives me a sense of detachment. There are purple pansies in the window box and the light from the sitting room window sends a soft glow into the dusk. It looks very cosy in there. I find myself thinking – do I really live in that house? I need to travel nowhere else for refreshment now; I just have to sit in different places and look in different directions to get a new view of things. Can I explain this to those who ask me why I never want to go away?

Chapter 3
JULY

Of MOVEMENT, paths and the Celtic Tree Calender.

'Surely I have traced
The rustle of those ample skirts about
These grassy solitudes, and seen the
flowers
Lift up their heads.'

John Keats – Hyperion.

Flowers and trees grow in different ways. Look at an oak tree and you can see how slowly it does it by the way the short twigs change direction every year and form a dense filigree of stiff branches. Compare it with a willow; those long graceful fronds, stretching towards the water, grow six feet in a season. I was told that if a willow cannot be planted close to a pond, a bucket of water placed under it will double the pace of its growth. Mine shot up into a swaying green canopy, completely enclosing the pond and the seat beside it, in five years.

Now I have to cut its hair every year.

At this time of year I can see the way things have grown. The irises sent up their great green swords very fast; they stand tall and erect until the winds get to them. Then they bend in into marvellous lapsed knife edges, dipping over the water to touch equally dramatic reflections, or twirl suddenly like mechanized toys, catching a breeze when nothing else is moving. Such forceful shapes contrast well with a delicate, arching fuchsia, the soft, new growth weighed down by dainty flowers. The globe artichokes jagged grey leaves curl under their own weight to a perfect point, yet the globes are held erect on strong, straight stems. Stonecrop creeps sideways, supported by the rock, forming dense cushions; nasturtiums climb and trail through other things for support and their flowers appear unexpectedly far away from where the seed germinated. Like dancers, growing things are influenced by their weight and strength and some need supporting with stakes and string. A landscape garden friend, talking about 'sculptural vegetation', advised me to plant something with big leaves between the broom and the red currant beside the stream. I nearly did, and then changed my mind and put a slender flower which leans out gracefully over the stream from between the two rounded bushes. Why? Maybe because it was its movement, the way it grows which creates a pleasing contrast, rather than the size and shape of its leaves. All this dancing sculpture changes from week to week and day to day, emphasized by shadows which are always on the move. So it is no wonder that, in such complexity, accidental combinations sometimes turn out better than plans. This month things need cutting back and shaping – the green sculpture of July. I shave grey foliage, which provides so much of the basic shapes in this garden, once the flowers are over, otherwise they get too big, hiding the stream and overwhelming stone walls. The flowering hedges – escallonia, broom and rosemary, need clipping too; so does the more fearsome boundary hedge. It is easy to pop in a few cuttings at the same time. I dig out brambles, nettles and knotweed; hack back hazel, wild plum, blackthorn and ivy. Long grass has to be cut with the strimmer and the lovely contrasts of mown paths wandering through waving long grass are lost. Burrowing under overgrown shrubs with secateurs produces mysterious caverns of shade against which any small flower, hidden by leaves, can be transformed by light. Perhaps it is as well that there are some vegetables to eat by now, because July can be a disappointing month. Once the roses drop, I am ashamed to say, I become bored by green. This is why I plant so many things with grey, silver or purple leaves.

My experienced friend was astonished at the strange collection of plants I had accumulated. He seemed to like the garden but it surprised him by its lack of any one style. Apparently I had mixed Mediterranean (grey leaves and *Pelargoniums*) with English Cottage (daisies and buddlea); natural rocks, pine, cistus and climbing roses (Country House) with Welsh fields, hills and woods, in a rather startling manner. As I was not in the habit of reading gardening magazines, I was ignorant of current style anyway. However, he approved of the smoke bush, seen through the rose arch, which catches the last rays of the setting sun. I explained that I had planted whatever I could beg, steal or propagate, in positions where, by trial and error, they would thrive. I was grateful for several suggestions he gave me on how to improve things and we drew up a list of plant movements that should take place in the autumn. It seems that the garden has reached stage two – it is full to overflowing with anything that turned up and now it needs some selective re-organization. We are always warned about this, but I would rather fill it up quickly and then sort it out later than spend five years weeding bare earth and waiting for the gaps to fill up. The element of surprise is part of the fun.

Stone walls produce wonderful accidents. Pennywort sprouts from the old lime plaster, its coin like leaves suddenly eject pale tongues of tiny bells that punctuate the hard surfaces throughout the summer. I discovered from a neighbour that these leaves, pulverized with butter or marge and spread over the skin, are a cure for shingles. herb robert trails everywhere; foxgloves seed themselves in all the right places, advancing like an army year after year, to invade different parts of the garden and decorate doorways, arches, steps and empty corners. I encourage them by never pulling them out. The yellow and orange Welsh poppies are also directing their own invasions.

I doubt if I will ever have the heart to cut down any of the trees that were once little saplings in my pocket. The ash have produced many pairs of regular branches which have already turned up their black tipped winter twigs like the fingers of Balinese dancers. The birch is already too big for the lawn but we need its branches for the hammock and its bright little leaves sparkle against the sky.

A garden is a series of pictures viewed from different places. When you look at a picture your eyes move in and out, from left to right and up and down, led by various devices. Perspective and scale, light and shade, the direction and quality of lines and edges, the combinations and intensity of colours – all these affect the way we respond to what we see. It is unsatisfactory to be led out of the picture and not back in again. Somewhere there needs to be a place to which the eye returns and rests – a focal point. This could be a tree, a bird table, a statue, a seat, a table, a sundial or something special like a standard rose. Or it could be the place where a path disappears around the corner, inviting you to go and investigate.

You can step into these pictures, move through them and let them change; or you can sit and gaze at a static view, imagine yourself moving or simply sit and stare. I have a view from the kitchen window that includes the first spring flowers; another at the top of the garden for summer evenings when the sun has left the lawn. I cut a hole in the hedge so I could see the sea shore, three miles away, from the sink. I cut a winding path up the grass bank towards the wood, intending it to be a short cut, and often travel it by eye, but hardly ever go that way. However, the geese do, every morning.

Even in the stillness of a Zen garden, there is move-ment. The eye is drawn towards mystery. What is be-yond? Your gaze may rest on the still surface of reflec-tive water and a fish jumps. A flat area of gravel is raked into curves like waves; carefully placed rocks become islands in an ocean; there are waterfalls, bridges and the graceful shapes of willow, pines and bamboo; step-ping stones lead you round a corner or into deep shade. This magical willow Pattern landscape was perfected by many generations of designers whose intentions were to create peaceful places where people could retreat from the noise and stresses of city life.

At dawn, when the mist still lies along the river, the val-ley is at its most mysterious. Trees appear and disappear

like soldiers without legs; hedges and woods pop up like cut outs in a child's picture book; misty hills seem to be breathing. The garden is a small part of this landscape so I try to make it fit, reflect the mystery by winding in and out like a Celtic knot, with lost and found edges. I want it to lead you into the picture, tempt you to go and look behind a bush, round the corner, through the gate, under the arch and up the steps until you find a spot where you would like to stay awhile, rest, gaze and dream, and feel better for it.

Children will show you where to go. They know paths were made for them – they follow them, taking off round trees, flower beds and ponds just to get to the other side. If there is anywhere to go they will set off, even in the smallest garden. There is something hypnotic about paths. The Zen gardener made footsteps for you – by placing flat stones set in turf at just the right distance to fit your stride; or boulders of diminishing size to create the illusion of distance in a small space. Paths can be made of many things. Brick lasts ages and grows attractive moss in time; gravel is tidy, stone slabs are beautifully solid; concrete, slate, cinders, wood chippings or grass – it depends on funds and labour available. They can be engineered like a Roman road, but I laid black plastic and covered it with broken slates, rubble and small stones collected from the cultivated beds and the chicken run. This kept weeds at bay and lasted several years. A swathe of short grass through an area of untamed vegetation makes an inviting way through a field or a wood and you can plant flowering bulbs or the occasional shrub along the edges. However small the garden, it is worth obscuring a bit of it, so there is somewhere to go to, something to discover round the corner.

There is an old track through my garden, cut out of
the rocks and worn smooth by hundreds of years of iron
shod cart wheels and horses, hob nailed boots and the
massed hooves of cattle and sheep. I was jubilant when
the District Council told me it was a public right of way
because it meant that my boundary, which had been for-
tified by barbed wire across the track, was opened up
again on both sides. New gates were provided by the National Park and we could walk in both directions without obstruction. There are wonderful views from this
old way, as there always are from most ancient routes.
They knew the best way to go when they travelled on
foot – shelter and a wide prospect with as little climbing
as possible. I put another seat beside this path for tired
walkers but few come by and fewer dare sit down. Their
experience of private land and nervous owners may not
have been encouraging. One of the Welsh Triads, which
embody the traditional lore of the Cymry, states, 'There
are three things, and any who move them are accursed;
the boundary of land, the course of water and the sign
of a road or track.' This track is still not signed, but at
least it is open again.

The very best kind of movement in a garden is running water. In other gardens I had tried to create it with
pipes and pumps but there is nothing like the real thing.
You only have to travel for a few weeks in a dry land
to realise why water, and its sources, became a focus of
worship in most cultures. Many of the rivers of Britain
still have their Celtic names and some secret wells and
springs are still decorated with old rags as they were before the Romans came. My Welsh garden began with
the unblocking of its spring.

The first years were dry ones and I worked all the year

round moving earth and water to establish the shape of the garden. Then, one day, when I was resting under the young willow beside the spring I realised that it could also happen here – the stream could dry up. I remembered the sight of dead villages in the Himalayas where this had happened – a fan of terraces, once a brilliant green, now faded to the pale pinks and greys of earth and rock without moisture, the remains of stone walls and mud houses white as bone, deserted. These were in places where it rarely rained and soil had to be irrigated from the melting snows in order to grow anything. Here the stream was already reduced to a trickle, all the Welsh reservoirs were low, their exposed shores edged with white. Where would the cities of Liverpool, Manchester and Birmingham be without Welsh water? The hills were yellow where the thin turf had died on the rock, the cattle panting in the meadow, the pond cracked and dry. In India I had understood the miracle of rain, but here we have taken it for granted for so long. Not so the ancient Celts, who left votive offerings at the sources of rivers. They understood, as did the Bronze Age farmers and metal workers who once lived on these hills and made offerings of their most prized possessions to the spirits of lakes and rivers. I was inspired by a photograph of one of the many votive offerings found in Source-Seine in the Massif Central – a slim female figure, crudely carved, hardly more than the form of the wood itself. I chose a piece of ash which already suggested the shape, carved it with a penknife, sitting in the sun on summer evenings. She was ready, by the Autumn Equinox, to take her place as guardian of the stream. I named her Sulis – the goddess of water. Now she looks as if she had grown there, green with moss, standing in the shadows among ferns and foxgloves, under the first tree I planted – the weeping willow.

In Welsh legend the salmon lies in the pool to catch the secret nuts of wisdom that fall from nine sacred hazel trees. I had planted a row of nut trees to screen the pool without counting them – there were nine. I had also planted birch, ash, alder, willow, oak, ilex, apple and rowan before I discovered that the first six, with hazel, were the seven sacred trees representing the days of the week in the Celtic Tree Calender of thirteen lunar months. Robert Graves, the poet, maintained that these thirteen trees – the first seven plus rowan, hawthorn, elder, bramble, ivy and broom, also represented the thirteen consonants of an ancient Gaelic alphabet. The five vowel sounds were represented by pine, gorse, heather, yew and poplar, with an extra letter Z for blackthorn. These symbols were not written down but, later, the Ogam alphabet was developed, which included five more sounds and used groups of strokes that could be carved into the vertical corners of posts or standing stones. These memorial stones can still be seen in many parts of Wales and Ireland.

So all these indigenous trees were already in the garden, or I had introduced them. I was pleased to discover that the magical time at the beginning of May was represented by Saille, the willow, the yellow moon tree, under which all this tree rambling began. Trees were sacred to the Druids – a Derwydd, or oak seer, was supposed to be able to transform trees into warriors and send them into battle. This idea might have something to do with the power of words and naming. When the name of god or goddess was secret only initiates were able to use the alphabet. Esoteric wisdom had been learned by heart and passed on orally; there was something dangerous about the written word; it could be interpreted wrongly by people who were not initiates. So there is this strange symbolic link between language and trees. The Battle of the Trees (Cad Goddeau), the poem Robert Graves 'decoded', concealed these intriguing nuts of wisdom in verse and riddles which were handed down orally for generations and only written down hundreds of years later. Since they have to be swallowed by the magic fish and transformed several times, it is no wonder we find it hard to interpret what it was our ancestors valued so much that they protected it with this symbolic army of trees. However, it is re-assuring that the same twenty trees of that old alphabet, which also included symbolic relationships to days and seasons, colours, familiar animals and birds, those guardians of more than words, are growing in this garden today.

Chapter 4
AUGUST

Of CHILDREN, colour, cuttings, birds and the end of summer.

'Your children are not your children.
They are the sons and daughters of Life's longing
for itself...
You may give them your love but not your thoughts,
For they have their own thoughts.
You may house their bodies but not their souls,
For their souls dwell in the house of tomorrow,
which you cannot visit, not even in your dreams.'

From 'The Prophet' by Kahil Gibran

My earliest memories are of my parents' garden. I remember being face to face with daffodils. Apparently, as soon as I could walk, I disappeared among the tall fronds of the asparagus bed, or mingled with Michaelmas daisies, hollyhocks or red hot pokers; Later I was overheard asking questions, presumably of the flowers since there was no one else around, 'Who are you? Can you hear me? Are you in there?'

My mother and father were dedicated to their garden; together they transformed three acres of field into a paradise in which we played for eight years. Then we had to leave. Many years later I returned to find a field again, but under the turf I could still feel the hard brick paths my father had laid in his circular rose garden where my brother and I had been parked in those high prams with fringed sunshades.

I hope my grandchildren, who live in cities, will collect some of their earliest impressions of the world from this garden. I often have them in mind as I make it, but I sometimes underestimate the physical effects of children on a garden. The gates, made to control the movements of ducks and geese, come off their hinges; delicate plants disappear; the smooth round beach pebbles collected to edge the pond are thrown into it; ducks die of fright; chickens escape and dig up vegetables; branches snap off young trees and brightly coloured plastic toys, shoes, balloons, balls and stuffed animals re-appear all over the place throughout the winter.

Some things are specifically for the children. A gnarled ash tree in the orchard has become an ideal site for the tree house, with rope ladder, swing and hammock. A rusty scaffolding tower, set up on the lawn, together with a couple of boards, an old climbing rope and some big cushions, keeps them occupied for hours, while we can keep watch from our chairs. The same is true of the ponds, which are used for paddling and fishing. One afternoon they caught the same unfortunate newt six times. Even so, a real child fishing in a garden pond is so much better than a bronze one. Children fit themselves

into the spaces in a rewarding manner; they follow the paths; sit on the seats; squat beside the stone lion and make nests in trees and under bushes. I shall always remember two naked babies lying on a rug in the flickering shade of the birch tree one hot summer day. The girl managed to roll right over, stretching her hand towards a bright nasturtium flower. Discovering herself so close to her companion, she grabbed hold of his private parts instead. This year she stands as high as the yellow flags round the pond and takes part in the female rituals. Three little girls in long skirts and floppy hats from the dressing up box are gossiping behind the rambling roses while the boys hurl themselves noisily from the top of the climbing frame onto the cushions.

Sometimes they all chase each other round and round the island bed that screens the seat, screaming; at other times they set off, silent and serious, to hunt for insects with magnifying glass and matchboxes, one behind the other, tramping the steep path and climbing the steps towards wilder places. Sometimes I see one alone and intent, face to face with a flower or gazing at something wriggling in the pond and I know that the old magic is still at work.

One very hot day during our second summer, when the children retreated from the garden with the cat and lay down on the cool slates of the kitchen floor, I realised that there was no shade outside. Nothing had grown big enough yet to cast a really cool shadow, so I planted a crab apple tree on the terrace. It is just big enough to cast a puddle of shade and not too large to block the view. It has blossom in the spring, then little red apples and I keep it cut back to a nursery rhyme shape.

Since I came to live in Wales four new babies have

been born; so now there are six grandchildren when the three families come for high days and holidays. It was because the family was increasing that I needed a bigger house. At the stage when many people are downsizing I did the opposite, with the hope that, if there was a spacious place to gather in, the children and my friends would come to visit. And they do. Although this was what I hoped would happen I had underestimated the levels of energy it would require. I had just become used to a slower pace of life, to solitude – so I found it hard to keep up with them. When they come and go, these sudden changes of life style and pace take some getting used to. As grandmothers, we have to learn how to let it flow along and not try to control anything, except ourselves. We do not have to do so much for these toddlers as we did for our own, although we try to when the parents look so exhausted. I am trying to relax into it, to sit in a chair and let them come to me instead of running around fetching and carrying things for them. Last summer I had so many visitors that when September came, I realised I had not had a solitary night since May. It took a week to recover. This year I managed better; I skipped family breakfasts and so preserved the essential daily portion of peace. When they have all gone and I miss them so much, I do all the strenuous jobs I put off when they are here and the hard work helps me to shift into solitude again. Every year the seasons slip by faster.

August.

There is a happy hum in the garden today, the sounds of summer – bees and water and the voices of children playing in the tree house or the pond; the parents chatting in the kitchen and on the terrace. I shall miss them so much next week. Could I cope if they were here all the time? I doubt it.

There are moments when everything runs together in transparent layers. Today we lay on the river bank and watched the water flowing over stones in dappled sunlight. So many colours gleamed from the river bed – pink, purple, orange, blue and the white quartz white pebbles polished by water – all the remnants of volcanoes that contorted this land five hundred million years ago. The water is crystal clear; its surface reflects the sky and turns into iridescent purple where the pink roots of willow wave across it. Under the bank it is black as night, but bubbles whirl through like shooting stars, or spiral over rocks to be sucked into galaxies of foam and spray. Caught on the bottom one brilliant emerald green leaf flickered like a starboard light. By softening my focus I saw all this at once – ourselves stretched out there together transfixed by the movement of water, the river in translucent layers, like time, most of it sweeping by, something held still in that moment.

Now, sitting in the garden again, this is how it feels as I listen to the hum of life around me – a background of flowers, cloud shadows, voices. A child dashes by, ducks splash in the pond and I am back in another time – my childhood, their childhood. All of us here now, generations flowing like that river into the future. A beam of consciousness can hold it for a moment, like that leaf glimpsed through layers of light in that moving river, holding beauty, intimacy, wonder, gladness – and then moves on.

We drink elderflower wine; we pick beans, courgettes, potatoes and collect eggs; we make a summer pudding with blackcurrants and raspberries. And then, after four long weeks of incubation, a proud mother duck leads twelve ducklings to water for the first time. How can such a tiny scrap of fluff paddle across the pond so soon after emerging from an egg?

This is the month when my colour schemes seem to break down and shapes disappear in heaps of indeterminate green. Huge weeds should not be allowed to seed, but this is also the month for relaxation, so they often get away with it. The meadow, with its second crop of silage, is so green it seems to give out emerald light after rain; the lawn also, but I connect its richness with a blocked lawn mower and too many loads of grass cuttings. If July and August are months of monsoon, as they often are, the summer visitors think it always rains in Wales. They may not discover our secret weather – the heat waves of May and the long, golden days of Indian summer in September.

Colour is subjective and every one has their preferences. In this Welsh landscape, with its grey rock, misty blue distances and sea breezes, grey foliage is at home. The pinks of mallow, cistus and old roses go well with the greys. I like purple and dark red with pink; blue next to purple; white with grey – white adds sparkle to everything. Bright reds and oranges that look so good against white walls in hot countries, do not seem to work so well here and this is the problem with August when the vivid flames of monbretia or nasturtiums thrive but do not settle with the more subtle hues of lavender or hebe. So I make notes to remind myself of what to do in the autumn. 'Move all the blue things into the little bed by the septic tank path; move the evening primroses

to the back of the border; scatter nasturtium seeds on
the rubble in the yard; move the dahlias away from the
mallow; plant mallow cuttings by the front gate; find a
better place for the yucca; dig the bluebells out of the
hedge and plant them under the ash tree; move orange
potentilla to top bank; separate the wild primroses from
the crimson primulas and plant them by the stream.'
You think you will remember, but you don't, because
something else happens next month to blot out the con-
clusions you came to and there are over six months of
colour combinations to consider.

Yellow is the colour of spring, with the bright new
greens. I have some lovely yellow polyanthus by the pond
which flower all through the winter and into spring,
when there are daffodils everywhere. But I do not want
yellow with the pinks and purples and blues in summer.
I am still trying to establish a blue bed, which I dreamed
of, but blue flowers are often delicate and I have not
succeeded yet. Evergreens make a good background for
spring bulbs so I have planted rhododendrons among
the trees at the back of the house and escallonia cuttings to make a boundary hedge to replace the awful
knotweed.

I have often wondered how people plan from a catalogue and plant all at once. It is difficult to imagine, apart
from the expense. My garden has had to grow gradually
and has been a process of trial and error. When something works, or arrives by itself I leave it. If it doesn't I
change it. It is a bit like scattering coloured cushions on
a sofa and moving them around until they agree. White
is wonderful – the star like heads of daisies sprinkled in
the border; drifts of white roses gleaming in the dusk;
delicate droplets of lily of the valley or white daffodils

after rain. Leaves should not be forgotten – grey leaves textured like velvet or old lace with the shimmer of a dark green rose leaf; the vivid spikes of lime green iris leaves against the dark hedge; translucent vine leaves, green turning to gold against a blue sky. Leaves come in so many shapes, sizes and textures they can be exciting at all times of year. Flowers come as a bonus.

Every one has their own favourites, so plant what you and your garden like best. Then add what goes well with what does well. I put a graceful hardy dark red fuschia in front of a purple hebe which flowers almost all the year round among rocks beside the pond. Then I found some sweet William plants that had been abandoned by a garden centre and popped them in the damp soil by the rocks. A year later their brilliant crimson flowers appeared through some self seeded herb robert – a wonderful accidental combination that remained in flower for months. The accidents are often more beautiful than any carefully made plan.

Local plants do better than those tiny bits and pieces that arrive by post and are inclined to wither in real soil. I get sudden ideas – I need something spiky here, or something to climb there, so I order something from a catalogue. But usually it is the anonymous green things some kind person brings me from a garden round the corner that settle down well and bear the best flowers or fruit, even if it is a year before I know what they will turn into.

Once you have discovered what suits your garden, you can propagate your favourites by taking cuttings. From June until October I pull off small side shoots from shrubs and some perennial flowers, mine or other peoples', leaving a heel at the end, remove some of the leaves, dip each one in water and rooting powder and push it down deep into loosened soil, preferably close to a solid edge so I can firm it down, either in a pot or against a rock or brick. They need to be watered well and put somewhere where they won't get lost or forgotten. When they sprout you know they are alive and forming roots so you can transplant them. Some sprout quite quickly, others seem to have died and then suddenly produce a flower. Rose cutting need to be left alone for at least a year and labelled or you forget what they are and where to put them. Most of my shrubs and several roses were grown like this. I take at least three at a time – a waxing moon may help. I tried doing clever things with razor blades and polythene, as seen on television, but found the outdoor cuttings did best. If the weather is very dry, or you go away, you can put a plastic bottle of water with a small hole in it nearby to drip onto your sapling trees or baby shrubs while you lie on a beach somewhere else. In winter straw or bracken will protect them from frost. Then one day, when you have forgotten all about them, you may find them in flower.

Every year more butterflies and bees come to the garden. The buddlea attract splendid red admirals, tortoiseshell and peacocks which feed here all through August. When I walk by the wild marjoram, collected from a Wiltshire chalk pit, hundreds of little brown butterflies rise like autumn leaves on a warm breeze and flutter round my head. I don't remember seeing so many since I was a child. And the ivy in the orchard hums with all kinds of bees.

It is five years since I first started to plant things here and make ponds. Since then various creatures have moved in – newts, butterflies, dragonflies and frogs.

Poultry food and compost heaps have attracted squirrels and rats and the poultry are a temptation to stoats,
weasels, mink, foxes and badgers. Others have departed.
I have not seen the tree creeper recently and the red kites
only visit on auspicious days. Sheep mustering in May
and building work next door have discouraged them
from nesting in the wood. When the kite does come, I
down tools and watch its spell-binding flight, but, all too
often, a buzzard or a raven will see it off. The latest new
arrival is a grey wagtail. In spite of the cat, there are
plenty of garden birds – robins, thrushes, blackbirds,
sparrows, wrens, and tits. Jackdaws nest in the chimneys
and the wood houses rooks, ravens, crows, pheasants,
woodpeckers, owls, pigeons, magpies and jays. I occasionally hear a cuckoo across the valley and the swallows return faithfully each year to nest in the barns. The
house martins gave up when the cat took to sitting on the
landing window sill. The heron sometimes visits the mill
pond next door and yellow hammers, goldfinches, long
tailed tits and redstart are occasional visitors.

For two years before I moved in, while the house was
let, I used to come up with the car full of tiny seedling
trees, collected from the woods in my pockets, cuttings
from roses, shrubs, bulbs and anything I could lay my
hands on to give the garden a start. One of those roses
is now scrambling all over the barn; the weeping willow
is a tree and those cuttings – flowering currant, mallow,
hebe, lupin, escallonia, ceanothus and cistus – have become great bushes.

August 30th 1989.
  *I arrived in a heat wave – warm seas, blue skies
and swallows. The stone buildings seemed to wel-*

come me in like arms. Everything is humming with heat – insects in the ivy, bees in the lavender, a breeze in the oaks. The car is bursting with 'boscage' – pots, boxes and bags of uprooted plants, shrubs and trees; cuttings wrapped in wet newspaper and polythene, or in pots I buried last year. Unable to move house quite yet, I am moving the garden instead. I have spent rapturous hours finding or creating homes for all these green things. I have built retaining walls of stone and filled them with earth because there is not much soil on top of the sloping rock. There seems to have been no rain for months so I visit the trees with a watering can every evening, returning from a swim in the sea, relaxed after a hardworking day by floating in the coloured path of the setting sun. I have improvised a seat where I eat my lunch and make plans. Bit by bit it takes shape. Plants know where to go now – they appreciate being consulted. I am re-using everything I dig up – slate, stone, brick and old iron. I make compost piles of weeds. The terrace takes shape, then the waterfall, then the stream diversion. I get carried away and miss my swim because I am too tired and hungry when I stop. The stream is flowing steadily in its course, filling both ponds and overflowing nicely into the ditch. Having reached a temporary completion outside I begin to investigate an old fireplace inside. This produces more stone... and so it goes on. Luckily the tenants are as enthusiastic as I am and help when they can.

The weather is breaking, with storms and rain at night. Earth moving is over for this year. The swallows gather on the wires, darting in and out for the last time, imprinting their home on their young. Like me, they will return in the spring.

When the swallows prepare for their long journey to warmer places there is always a slight feeling of sadness, of ending, redolent of all those summers when the holidays were drawing to a close and it was time to get ready to go. It never got any easier, so this strong feeling remains like a smell, attached to the gathering of swallows. But now I no longer have to go. I am not in a holiday house, I live here now. The end of summer and the inevitable sadness of parting is cushioned by another feeling – a secret, triumphant kind of pleasure at becoming a permanent resident at last, after so many years as a visitor to Wales. Now I am looking forward to golden autumn days ahead; the weather always improves after the summer visitors have gone. The relief at being able to stay to enjoy it is enormous, like taking off a rucksack at the end of a long day's walk – you feel as if you are floating up off the ground as all the muscles relax. I no longer have to leave with the swallows.

Chapter 5
SEPTEMBER

Of solitude, HARVEST, muck and muscle and the Autumn Equinox.

> 'It is the wordless occupation
> that sets the mind busily at
> work'
>
> Delius

September brings solitude, and more time to get to grips with the accumulation of things that need doing in the garden. It is like changing gear, a necessary space, after months of sociability, in which to adjust to a new season. During these long, warm days of autumn, when the soil is still light and dry, there is nothing I would rather do than spend all day out of doors, attending to all the jobs I listed when there was no time to do them.

The village produce show, a harvest ritual, makes me take stock of things – polishing the best matching apples, saving the biggest dahlias and hydrangeas, picking sweet peas with the longest stalks and then gathering with other gardeners to admire each others' produce and celebrate the completion of another year. The prize leaks are as thick as my arm, with long green hair which falls from the table and flows across the floor; head sized onions, plaited and polished; ingenious model gardens in baking tins invented by children; giant marrows, cabbages, pumpkins, carrots and parsnips grown by magicians from seeds developed by their grandfathers, the secrets of propagation and care handed down the generations of the clan.

I cannot compete, except with apples. They are expected to look after themselves and, when everyone else has black-spot, my young trees excel. Or perhaps I can find four pansies or marigolds to display on a plate, or a bottle of home made wine, six fresh free range eggs or a jar of autumn chutney. There are so many classes and not many entries so most of the locals win something. I do not try to compete with the cakes or pastry; the secrets of successful baking are jealously guarded in a Welsh village, as are those of the vegetable giants. Competition can get quite heated and it is not a good idea for a newcomer to win the flower arranging either. But I love to see it all laid out on the long tables, being minutely inspected and compared by the growers – amateurs in the true sense of the word. Everything here has been grown with muck and muscle – and love.

Taking stock, I discover the garden is a mass of weeds which were allowed to get away with it while I was relaxing and romancing my way through summer. Now the wheelbarrow never gets put away; the pick, fork, bucket, shears, secateurs, scissors, string, wire cutters and wire come with me as I work my way round. A garden apron

with a big pocket, or a waistcoat with lots, is a help.
Heaps of rubbish outgrow their spaces; everything that
will burn is piled up in the yard where there is enough
room to celebrate Samhain or Guy Fawlkes safely. The
compost bins have to be emptied of their contents and
spread on the vegetable garden. Meanwhile the lawn
mowings and bonfire ash go on the soft fruit to keep the
weeds down. It is hard weeding between raspberries;
gooseberries are worse, because of the thorns. Nettles
come out best in dry weather and all those creeping
weeds like convolvulus, couch grass and ground elder,
buttercup and even dock come out better from loose
mulch than impacted earth. If the soil is too sticky, wait
for a better day, but get them out. These are the perennial weeds which just get worse, while annual weeds die
down and come out in handfuls. Brambles have been
thriving here for so long their root balls ares as big as
my fist and they grow fifteen feet in all directions each
year, rooting again on the way. It will take years to get rid
of them all. I would rather pick blackberries from other
peoples' hedges.

There is not so much left to eat in the garden now.
The beans, peas and potatoes have all been consumed.
I transplant baby artichokes which have taken five years
to get to this size; I fork over the beds, disentangling old
netting and pea sticks. All that is left is spinach, leaks, a
few courgettes, tomatoes trying to ripen, parsnips and
beetroot and the lacy leaves of the purple sprouting
broccoli that the caterpillars have enjoyed. They will recover by spring. If the weather is not too dry things can
be moved now. As I clear up the flowers beds I divide
things and find them new homes. Then it is all ready to
settle down for the winter.

Indian summer is a wonderful time of year. Time seems to stand still at the Equinox and the calm weather often continues until the clocks change. Before the winter routines of evening classes and meal sharing among neighbours, there comes a period of unstructured and uninterrupted days before the weather breaks. Every year I attack more long grass at the back. The turf is thin on the rock and water seeps through it most of the year. I can strip the rock bare in some places, when conditions are right, by rolling it up like a carpet and stacking it up to make more pockets of soil for bulbs. As the trees mature the grass dies back, replaced by ivy and woodland plants like wild garlic, I envisage a grassy path flanked by lavender, heather and rhododendrons, winding up to blue hydrangeas, eucalyptus and pines against a blue sky. It will take a while. After the August gales, the sea throws up seaweed. A friend helped me collect this from the beach. We piled it into old bread crates and dragged it up over rough shingle with a rope, loading smelly heaps into a trailer. By leaving it in a pile when it rains most of the salt is washed out, then it rots down and provides the soil with lots of nutrients. Potatoes in Cornwall and Pembrokeshire used to thrive on this; it may still be used in parts of Ireland.

Poultry and goats also provide manure. After scraping the floor of the shed with a hoe a good way to pick the stuff up is with two short lengths of plank which is easier than a shovel. I also lay old plastic sacks on the floor to catch the chicken droppings and then pull the whole lot out and onto the compost heap to rot down. Some of it can go into a covered water butt and next year it will be a rich liquid feed. I also do this with comfrey leaves and nettles. This foul smelling liquid takes about three months to mature and must be diluted with three parts of water, but it works well on tomatoes, pot plants and window boxes.

The sorting of kitchen rubbish provides endless amusement – five different categories and only one of them for collection. I find it easy as I have done it all my life, beginning with a frugal wartime childhood. The habit stuck, but my younger, city bred guests find it confusing, and funny. You need to know what will burn, what chickens will not eat, like citrus fruit or their own flesh; what will biodegrade, the difference between metal, plastic and glass and where to put it. Those brought up to put everything into one black bin bag find it all hilarious. 'Will chickens eat banana skin? Where should we put rice pudding? Old socks? Jelly babies? Felt tipped pens?' Even the difficult one, 'What about bones?' was solved when I discovered that the crows carry them all away at dawn. The same bones occasionally appear again indoors when the jackdaws try to build nests in the chimney. *Naturum expellas funca, tamen usque recurrent.* (You can throw out nature with a pitchfork but she will always turn up again).

Five years ago there was very little good soil in the garden. Every year, with the addition of compost and some farmyard muck, it improves. The vegetables are small but very tasty and they appear when we need them most, during the summer. Fresh garden produce has become an integral part of the holidays. Harvest time includes wild produce as well. During these sunny days I go in search of blackberries, crab apples, sloes and wild plums. All these were planted in the hedgerows hundreds of years ago and, no doubt, the children were sent to collect the fruits, as we were as children. We were

told not to return until the basket was filled with blackberries. Of course we complained, but we did it and I
think we enjoyed those days of late sunshine, scratched
legs and sticky fingers. Now I make jams and jellies and
chutney with anything left in the garden, particularly the
green tomatoes. The vine I planted outside the kitchen
has small bunches of tiny grapes, but it is a decorative
addition to the heaps of produce that accumulate on the
kitchen table.

Autumn brings out the hunter gatherer instincts.
Some years there are mushrooms to add to the riches
– big field ones, small white buttons, puff balls (before
they go puffy) and, occasionally, some chanterelle or
boletus at the edges of the woods. Squirrel like inclinations lead me to store away as much as possible for the
darker days to come. I love to see those shiny jars on the
larder shelves. I built a larder when I came here, just so
I could indulge these fancies. And jars of home made
things come in handy as presents. This is the place of
elders – the mountain is named after them. Now I race
the birds to get the berries for red wine, to drink hot and
spiced on winter evenings when the year has turned, in
the month of the elder – November. The elderflower
wine made in June cannot be drunk before Christmas,
so this wine fills a gap.

With Christmas looming, I sometimes make lavender
bags as presents from the flowers that have dried over
the Aga. These go on smelling all year and are a cure
for insomnia. Dried peppermint makes good tea which
soothes the digestion; camomile makes a good bedtime
drink. Rosemary trimmings make an excellent hair rinse
for dry hair and seems to slowdown the grey. Concocting
potions from plants must be in our genes, handed down

through generations of country grandmothers from the wise women who really knew about the healing properties of plants and were burnt because of it. All this is being re-discovered now, just in time before it gets lost. I feel I am in good company.

> *September 21 – Equinox*
>
> *Today has been calm, not a breath of wind and the sun warm. I sat in the garden with friends. They said that the garden has a special atmosphere, unlike other gardens. I asked in what way and the reply was, 'It is so peaceful here – a bit magical'. That was the best of compliments. During the summer an American visitor had said that the garden and surrounding land, 'stirred up unknown pagan connections' for her. The best definition of religion that I have come across – 'The ritual re-enforcement of existing connections' – was given by Gertrude Levy in 'The Gate of Horn' where she described the relationship between prehistoric people and the animals they hunted. Perhaps a loss of meaningful connections with the natural world brings a lack of religious experience, or feeling, although so many structures have been invented to replace it. I am glad my connection was made very early and maintained for long enough to become conscious. Then, when circumstances removed me from the kind of places I needed, although I pined for them, I never completely lost it. Now I am back in a familiar land, like a tree planted in the soil where it seeded, well rooted grows stronger. So, when the place works for other people too, my connection is strengthened although the rituals are private.*

This year the moon was not full at the Equinox, but soon after. On a clear calm evening it rose over the mountain as big and almost as red as the sun sinking into the sea in the opposite direction. This conjunction gives a rare sense of peace and balance, especially at this time of year. It was at such a time that I had first placed the guardian beside the stream and, after three years, she needed some attention. So I treated her with wood preservative and tidied up her base, which had begun to rot. Hundreds of insects fell out when I turned her upside down. Now she stands in a drain pipe with a hat to shield her from the rain. It was once the top of a stove chimney and makes her look a bit Chinese, so I think I will give her a second name – Kuan Yin. Her first name – Sulis – stolen by the Romans and converted into a sun god to guard the springs at Bath, became Sul or Sil, and appears quite often in Welsh place names connected to springs. Now, as Sulis Kuan Yin (Regarder of the Cries of the World) – Celtic goddess and female Buddha – she gazes down on the reflection of the full moon in the pool under the willow and at the foolishness of this world, with an amused and compassionate smile.

Chapter 6
OCTOBER

Of learning with ANIMALS and preparations for winter.

'See how it hangs on air.
The leaves are turning now. We cannot hear
The death and birth of life. But that disguise,
Look up now, softly; break it with your eyes.'

'The Turning of Leaves' – Vernon Watkins.

October.

I wake just before dawn and look out of the window. The mallow is still in bloom, making a soft, pink frame for the meadow – a green saucer floating on a low blanket of mist along the river. Those Druid armies, the trees, are coming through the mist, moving through layers of paler and paler blue, shape shifting in a legendary manner and dissolving into water vapour as the air grows warmer. I watch the sheep walking slowly across the meadow, following one another, until they are standing by the gate in a group, facing east. They remain, motionless for several minutes as the sun rises over the hill, casting their long shadows across the grass like Chinese brush strokes. When the light has reached their eyes they turn, one by one, and walk away to graze near the wood, like a congregation after mass, erasing their shadows as they go. Crows fly down to strut about between them, waiting for anything that might drop from the warmer wool. As the dawn breeze disperses the mist I can see the trees are no longer green. Dead leaves flutter down among the sheep.

Frogs greet the dawn too. I have seen them line up across the pond on a February morning to sing to the rising sun, their swollen white throats pulsating with music like a Welsh male voice choir. Animals and birds live regular lives; they thrive on routine and ritual. After a lifetime of trying, unsuccessfully, to make useful habits, I now find myself catching some from animals. I watch cormorants flying home in formation at the same time each evening with the crops full of fish; listen to rooks settling down in the oak wood across the valley; see the raven fly south as the aeroplane from London to New York sets out across the Irish Sea into the sunset. Then the gulls return to the sea, owls call and bats appear. As the autumn evening get chilly the ducks expect their evening meal earlier and earlier so I adapt to their rhythms. If I don't shut them up before nightfall they will set off for the safety of the mill pond next door and no amount of rattling of the grain tin will bring them back. I feel cosily smug as I put the kettle on, the evening animal rituals completed – I am making habits too.

Watching animal and birds can help us understand human nature. Step mothers and fathers having trouble getting along with their new mate's offspring might realise how much biology they contend with if they could see how it operates in the duck world. A protective mother duck attacks any duckling that does not belong to her and a drake attacks his own if they demand too much of his mate's attention, even though he has stood patiently beside her for four weeks of incubation. As soon as the eggs are hatched and the family take to water he is after her again. The young get in his way. A mother duck will even kill a weakling of her own, or ducklings of the wrong colour if she has too many to look after, or too little open water. A dozen seems to be too many, unlike a chicken, she cannot fluff out her feathers to keep them all warm and dry so, if some don't die of exposure in the first few days, she may try to get rid of the weaklings. Thus only the fittest survive.

Everyone attacks a runt. I had a duckling named Napoleon. He was hatched the right size but, at six weeks, was only half as big as his peers. From the beginning he did everything differently – as did my eldest grandson. He rushes about after flies instead of following obediently behind his mother; he swam in the wrong direction and got left behind at bed time; he hid in the bushes when the others were all lined up for grooming instruction. He was given such a hard time by his parents and siblings that I did not think he would survive, but then, one day, he became the leader of the ten that waddled home at night. One night soon after that, when the others spent the night out on the pond, he came home alone to the safety of the shed. Then I discovered that he was not a drake after all – she is a duck.

All this makes me wonder if a hard and lonely childhood is the breeding ground of a leader, or if the potential leader gets a hard time from parents and siblings until he or she is big enough to get back at them. The smallest has to be stronger to survive, so perhaps the habit of relentless struggle rakes them to the top where they can makeup for early persecution by wielding power later. One thing is clear – animals can have complicated relationships and suffer from traumas and conflicts which sometimes lead to neurosis just as we do, but less often maybe.

Before I became familiar with the needs and idiosyncrasies of ducks, they kept disappearing. Now I clip their wings, but this makes them more vulnerable to predators and dogs. I had a young cockerel who was being persecuted by his sire for developing a competitive interest in hens, so he left the orchard and began to roost on the roof, alone. He spent his days on the kitchen window sill, crowing a lot, and then he attached himself to a lonely drake who had lost his mate to the fox. For the whole of one winter they were inseparable, the cockerel finding food and calling to the drake to share it, standing back to let him eat just as he had tried to do with the hens. They made a splendid couple, the drake with his fluorescent green feathers and cock well preened and colourful. It wasn't until the spring came and the cockerel began to view the drake as his mate that I had to make new arrangements. When I acquired another duck and a few more hens they all settled down to a more normal life and began to breed. Lonely animals behave in strange ways. I had a gander once which had been left to fend for itself when its mate was killed by hunting dogs and its owner moved away. It was so traumatised it spent all day gazing at itself in the window, presumably thinking its reflection was its old mate. I fed it all one winter and felt so sorry for it I bought a young goose to keep it company, but even then it preferred its own reflection. I had to cover up the glass with hardboard before it would pair for a second time and breed again. In later years when the flock had increased in size and there was a young gander to compete with, the first one would sometimes return to the window for solace.

Sometimes I feel a sense of hopelessness when I watch animal behaviour, not for them but for us. Our biology does not always seem to help. A doctor once said to me, 'You realise, don't you, that once through the menopause, you are biologically useless?' We are still largely at the mercy of our basic instincts, to breed, defend our territory, fight our competitors and reject the weak. A duck is either breeding or dead, but our species, which has been walking the earth for over two million years, has other ambitions too. As far as we know, birth control has only become generally available for a few generations, although it is likely that our pastoral ancestors once regulated their affairs to fit in with seasonal necessities, just as some people living in remote areas may still do. Female biology may not have even adapted yet to walking upright; we would probably produce babies more easily if we walked miles every day and squatted on our heels, instead of sitting at desks and eating chocolate bars. Even children, who should be running around all day, or sound asleep like puppies if they are to develop strong hearts and limbs, sit down for half the day at school and then spend much of the rest of it in front of a flickering screen, which may be less beneficial than firelight was.

How can we expect human biology, which evolved gradually over so long for hunting and gathering, adapt suddenly to recent conditions? Economics, politics, academia and even psychiatry, which has been accused of coming into being to service the nuclear family, all underestimate the influence of human instincts, although religious moralists have found names for some of them. Unlike ants and bees, we are still evolving, so there is hope for us, unless we destroy our habitat. While our instincts still work as strongly as ever toward the survival of our species, regardless of others, they spike our efforts to transcend them. So, as our numbers increase, this works against us. Competition over territory, resources and women, has not changed much since the Bronze Age, when deteriorating weather forced people down from the hills to fight for land. More than three thousand years later the emphasis is once again on competition rather than co-operation. If we are too greedy, of course, our host may simply shrug us off. However, we have bitten the apple, we know things animals may not. We think the universe is infinite; we know we are going to die, and we also know there would be enough to go round on earth, if only we could find a way to share it. If we could accept our condition, not as lords of the earth but as a lucky form of life, we might develop ways of life based on our finer feelings.

Jan Morris, writing about Wales in terms of the four elements, says in her essay Dear (Earth) '... like the sun and the stars which played so compelling a part in the lives of the first inhabitants of Wales, the birds, the beasts, fish and insects are part of the grand community, essential to the pattern that contains night and day, hill and valley, land and sea, man and woman and God himself.' Animals link us to more than themselves. The cat is my teacher. When I rush about too fast, he trips me up; when I sit down he jumps on my lap and purrs. He sleeps when he is tired, insists when he needs something, welcomes me home, lies on his back when he wants to be friends and minds his own business. The animals tell me things about myself, the garden tells me things about the world. It thrives if I look and listen, pay attention to the way things work and work with them. A flower seeds itself in exactly the right place, or a person is suddenly able to understand something that has been obscure for years.

When I was a child most people I knew kept a few hens in the back garden; some people bred rabbits for meat and every farm had a couple of house pigs, fed on domestic food scraps. But chicken was a luxury then. All that changed; farming methods, which have turned chicken into cheap protein, have almost bred the broody habit out of hens. But, luckily, when they return to natural surroundings, with a cockerel, it returns. Each year one goes broody so there are a few new chicks to replace the old ones the foxes and badgers take. People find it hard to believe that badgers kill and eat poultry. But, since they were protected, they have bred so successfully that they have had to change their diet in order to survive. When the bracken dies down we can see their motorways between the set and toilet areas. They get under walls and fence, foxes climb over. One solution, still in the experimental stage, is to line the boundary with little heaps of lion dung from the local zoo. The smell is so appalling it is supposed to scare everything away.

The chickens roost in the old pig stye, getting in and out by a ladder, which deters badgers and foxes, although squirrels soon learned to climb it and steel the corn. The egg boxes are built into the wall just under the eaves, so we do not have to bend down to collect eggs. They soon learn to lay in the right place if it is well insulated – chickens hate draughts. They free range in the orchard, scratching up worms and insects to improve the taste of the eggs; they make themselves dust baths and drink from the stream. Unlike some domestic ducks, East Indian Blacks will sometimes sit and hatch their own eggs. They are fragile creatures but a wonderful addition to the garden. They do not scratch up flowers or make much mess and they create continuous decorative diversions and entertainments on the pond, their superb green and purple plumage shining like gems in the sun. When I open the garden gate they always greet me with frenzied quacking and they come home faithfully when called at night. Some people do not shut up their ducks by night and rely on water to protect them, but we have too many predators here and do not want to loose them. Wild ducklings have a very low survival rate.

Geese only need feeding in winter if they have plenty of grass, but I feed mine to entice them in at night. They need a decent pond to swim in, and to mate successfully because they are heavy birds. Gentle creatures, except when guarding their young, they keep down rough grass and make plenty of noise at the approach of strangers. Although they prefer to pair for life they are happiest in flocks of four or more and become quite interesting when you get to know them.

While the property next door was empty I was able to keep two goats. A really good, high fence and a reasonable shelter from wind and rain are essentials, but they are easy to feed because they chew up almost anything.

A lone goat will wander looking for company so I had two – brother and sister who had always been together – a gentle nanny called Honey and her de-horned brother called Ginger. They were adorable, funny, affectionate and very intelligent. Luckily they were so contented together they did not try to roam and they loved human company, particularly of children.

One October morning, when I went to let them out of their stockade, I was amazed to see two strange, mythical beasts, trying to break into it. These animals had huge, spiralling horns, and silky brown and white hair reaching almost to the ground. Taking turns they were systematically battering one of the corner posts with their heads, running at it from a distance of several yards. When they saw me they raised their heads and stared fearlessly with wicked yellow eyes. I wondered if I were dreaming – these were creatures from a legend – and I was afraid of them. The smell was awful and Honey stood in the far corner, quivering. Ginger was hiding in the shed, being totally unequipped for such competition. They were wild, feral goats from a small group which have occupied a nearby mountain for a thousand years or so.

It took me a while to decide what to do; I needed help, so I rang a local farmer who came immediately with a young shepherd and a dog. The dog was terrified and it took over an hour to round them up. When we cornered them they climbed a stone wall, ran easily over the barn roof and jumped fifteen feet down the other side. They jumped two more walls and several fences and raced away up the mountain. The intrepid shepherd followed and, eventually, one was captured with a flying rugger tackle and the other tangled its horns in a fence. Both were tied with binder twine and flung in the back of the Land Rover, to be returned to their mountain. The awful cry they gave at this indignity made me wish I'd let them stay.

There was an unexpected sequel to this story. One evening the following March it was almost dark when I called in the goats. They were hungry and came running. When I had shut the door I almost fell over three tiny lambs curled up by the fence. Where was their mother? I carried them back to the field hoping the ewe would find them. No sheep showed any interest when they began to bleat pathetically. The goats were bleating too, so, to keep them warm, I changed my mind and put them in with the goats for the night. By torchlight I saw that Honey had the remains of the afterbirth – they were hers. I was so astonished I spent the next hour watching her lick and feed them. Three long legged, short tailed creatures – how had I mistaken them for lambs? How on earth had she carried them all without my noticing? Now she was as thin as a rake and ravenously hungry. I fetched more food, dry bedding and water and left them for the night.

The whole episode had the quality of an immaculate conception – she could not have mated, Ginger was doctored. I was wrong, of course. I counted the months – somehow those two mythical billies had got inside the stockade after all. The story was round the village like wildfire. People came to visit and marvel at the three splendid kids; children came to play with them. I was told the nanny could not feed all three, especially as they would soon grow horns. But she did. The family grazed and sunbathed through the summer, then I was lucky to find someone to take the whole family. Recent EU regulations meant the local abattoir had such a restricted quota it could not take goats. The alternative was worrying – if I advertised them they would probably go to a midland city for ritual slaughter. The man who bought them had come for geese, but when he saw the five together he fell in love with them and decided to buy them instead. He reckoned they would teach his fourteen prize goats to eat grass. I was sad to see them go, they had become a part of my life, but when they hopped obediently into the back of the van and settled down together on the straw I was very relieved to have found them a good home. A week after they went, the agent wrote to tell me I must move the goats because the mill was up for sale – serendipity had worked once more.

> *October.*
>
> *Everyday the trees change colour a little. We have had rain but not much wind so the oaks have kept their leaves. In the garden the late sunshine has meant the roses are in flower again. Fresh pink buds keep appearing on the albertine which is supposed only to flower once. The ceanothus seems to think it is spring too, although the sky is clear and I can smell frost. Last night I covered the cuttings with straw and brought the potted geraniums inside. There are still a few bats about. I have planted dozens of crocus under the silver birch by the top seat, hoping that this time the mice will not eat them and the delicate mauve mist I dream of will materialize next spring. The eucalyptus have been pruned, as advised, to help the root system grip the thin soil. They have grown several feet in their first year.*
>
> *I managed to get hold of a bale of straw, which is hard to come by here, and returned the geese to their*

winter quarters. Free ranging during the summer they had become rather wild and one flew away on the wind to the river. Although they have been calling to each other it seems unable to fly uphill. When I went to look for it I found it swimming with a family of swans. I hope it will find enough to eat during the winter and that they will protect it from Christmas predators.

Today it is still warm enough to sit outside at lunchtime, watching the garden gleam and sway in golden light, listening to the swollen stream and the bees feeding in the ivy. Five swans flew in a circle over the river, low light catching their wings and the crimson vegetation along the banks. I do hope they will stay with that goose. All lines are horizontal today, shadow, hedges, distant woods, the edge of land where it meets the sea and pale streaks across the sky. Now I shall be away for two weeks, but the garden is ready for winter and there is a huge heap of rubbish ready to burn when the children come next month. Tonight is cold enough for the first frost and a pink crescent moon is hanging over the sea.

Chapter 7
NOVEMBER

Of Samhain, the ELEMENTS, pilgrimage and dreams

'Wind blew once till it seemed
the earth could be skinned from the
fields,
the hard roots bared.'

Jeremy Hooker.

November
The terrible north east wind is tearing down the valley. Three rams are huddled against the garden hedge and the mountain cattle, six cows with their calves and a big black bull, are cowering by the gate. It makes coming in and out by car quite tricky. This week has been so cold it feels as if every living thing has shrunk back into the underlying rock that shapes the landscape. Its colours faded to a grey green mono-tone when a hard frost wiped out every tenacious petal that had survived the gales. The last leaves let

go; the mallows shrivelled; the luscious green and orange nasturtiums disappeared overnight, reduced to a slimy heap; elegantly arched fuchsias turned into dead twigs waiting to be cut back to the root. Walking up the hill yesterday the wind was so strong it was hard to stand. I looked down on a valley filled with a strange light, made of windswept clouds pouring over the mountain and dissolving as they were blown towards the sea, filling spaces between rocks and trees with a solid kind of brilliance. Hillsides were obscured and flattened by this palpable light; it streamed in from the west, met the clouds and absorbed them, filling up the valley as if with liquid. It would have overflowed but the rocks held it in, their jagged dark purple edges cutting into the sky and exaggerating every detail of their making. Last night there was an eclipse of the moon, but it was hidden by racing cloud. This was disappointing; after a week of clear, frosty nights and brilliant moonlight I had hoped to watch it happen again, as I had years ago in the chalk country on May Day. Perhaps this strange, wild weather was something to do with the moon. Now the eclipse is over the wind has returned home to the south west and the land is grey again.

At Samhain, when the year turned, I was at Chartres. It is an extraordinary place. The river winds round a rocky knoll on which the Cathedral was built and, as you approach across the flat surrounding plain, this incredible bunch of spires appears in the sky like a dream palace floating on air. Bridges, winding ways and steep steps lead you through terraced gardens up and up until the massive bulk of its carved stonework leans

over you. Stepping inside is like entering a dim forest;
the pillars shoot up like tree trunks and disappear into
darkness. Brilliant streams of light break through a ka-
leidoscope of medieval stained glass and leave coloured
puddles on the stone floors, worn smooth by the feet of
countless pilgrims. Under one of the windows is the famous maze, a labyrinth of twelve windings, symbolizing
the journey of the soul. Originally, before the cathedral
was built, a cave in this rock housed an image of a virgin
goddess sacred to the Druids; now the shrine to Notre
Dame de la Belle-Verriere is always lit by hundreds of
candles and decorated with flowers.

The old autumn festival of Samhain took place at
the end of October, probably at the full moon. Bonfires
were lit as they are today, since Guy Fawkes, poor fellow,
became an excuse for a good burn up. There is always
a great heap of garden rubbish to burn at this time of
year. The word bonfire has come down to us from the
Stone Age bone fires, which were lit when animals were
slaughtered as grazing ran out. Samhain was one of the
oldest seasonal festivals; the others were Imbolc, the
coming of yews' milk in February; Beltaine, the spring
festival in May and Lughnasadh, or Lammas, harvest
in August. These four quarters, counted in moons, were
probably the first divisions of time to be marked by the
hunter gatherers and early farmers; equinoxes and sol-
stices came later, as attention shifted from the moon to
the sun and people began to work out the complex relationships between the movements of the sun, moon
and stars. Gradually, as Christian festivals replaced the
pagan ones, Samhain became All Souls Day, a time to
remember the dead. All Hallows Eve, or Hallowe'en,
acknowledges the older idea of the closeness of life and

death at this time of year, with ghost stories and grinning sculls. Our fire festival that year took place the weekend before the gales began. The heap of garden prunings had dried out well and everything was consumed.

In all ancient cultures the seasons, the elements and the features of the natural world obviously had religious significance; there are similarities to be found in beliefs from all over the world. The Celtic traditions are not easy to trace because continuity was broken by invasions and persecution, but there are echoes from other places. The old elemental gods and goddesses that symbolized the different ways of being were eventually incorporated into the all encompassing deity and qualities which once had individual powers of transformation faded into the mists of the western hills. Listen to Taliesin:

I have been many shapes
before I attained congenial form...

I know the star knowledge
Of stars before the earth was made,
Whence I was born,
How many worlds there are...

I have travelled over the earth
Before I became a learned person.
I have travelled, I have made the circuit,
I have slept in a hundred islands;
I have dwelt in a hundred cities.

In Tibetan Buddhism, where traditional wisdom and practices have been handed on almost without interruption for thousands of years, the elements – earth, water, fire, air and space – are still used as symbols in practical psychology. Fire, in the Tibetan system, is compulsive and obsessive. I recognize myself rushing about from one thing to another, burning up energy in excessive emotional reaction. Fiery people may feel isolated until they are able to let go of this consuming energy and let be. When fire energy transforms itself it can become compassionate, appropriate, discriminating and wise.

An earth based reaction is a kind of insecurity which has to do either with poverty or with pride and ownership. Once it is liberated this kind of energy becomes balanced and generous. A person who was busy buying and clinging onto things begins to give them away.

Water takes many forms; it is essential to life. It is powerful without being hard; in cloud form it can block out the sun; it wears away stone and puts out fire. It can be frightening; a storm at sea, a huge waterfall or a flood symbolizes the anger and aggression induced by fear. But a quiet lake is the most peaceful image of all and, if you stare into a mirror of still water, or ice, and see your face contorted by fury, you have to laugh. That is how you take your anger for a walk, from a furious force to a limpid lake; then it turns into clarity – insight.

Air is to do with anxiety and paranoia, a kind or formless panic. Someone in that state of mind should sit down for a minute, take a deep breath and decide where it hurts, and why. This kind of energy can be transformed into free activity and self-fulfilling action. You know the feeling when your heart leaps into your throat for no good reason; you see a pile of bills or unanswered letters – why do they make you feel afraid, as if someone were after you? Instead of rushing off to distract yourself by doing something else, stop and let that butterfly feeling overwhelm you. Try it. Something can spring inside, like a knot coming undone. Then, quite easily, not all screwed up with wilful determination or anxiety, you will find yourself doing whatever it was that needed to be done, like writing the letter that had been log jammed for weeks, quite easily. This sounds so simple but it is not always so easy to do. It helps to find out where the feeling actually is – in your stomach, your hands, your head or your heart. Once you discover that it is inclined to dissolve.

Then there is space. Space can be bewildering; it can cause depression and torpor, or it can become infinitely intelligent and sensitive. There are some spiritually advanced people, like Mother Teresa or the Dalai Lama, who have become so familiar with emptiness that they can talk for hours, unprompted and without a script, drawing on a depth of wisdom that answers all questions before they are asked. Mystics of many traditions have spoken from their experience of space – Lao Tsu, Kahil Gibran, Jesus, Buddha or Taliesin; as have artists, philosophers and poets. But many people are afraid of emptiness – it takes practice to discover the creativity that flows from internal space.

We are taught to hide our feelings from other people; we learn to do things to disguise and muffle them, to distract ourselves. Unfortunately this may also mean we loose touch with what we feel, and what we are. If we stop doing for a bit, let ourselves feel what is actually happening, and let it be what it is, we may find negative feelings pass more quickly.

In the Tibetan system the elements symbolize the energy of different kinds of emotion which can be used as powerful tools, if we can accept them and let them change. By trying to suppress or control them we block this natural movement. Depression, which is a kind of deadness, seems to be an accumulation of blocked feelings which can, eventually, lead to physical and emotional breakdown. Anything which stimulates physical sensation can help to bring feelings to life again, like a swim in the sea, strong wind, music or the smell of a rose. I can remember being told to 'Put something between yourself and the feeling!' so I would go and dig the garden when I was upset. I thought that was very clever; I did feel better, I dug it all in. No wonder I did not enjoy that garden. I now realise why I had to dig so deep years later to recover from the effects of all those burials.

* * *

November is not usually a gardening month although, during the first week, I may be picking the last roses and sweet peas. It is a good time to be considering the elements. The earth will soon be asleep, sheltering the fallen seeds; water pours out of the sky into streams and rivers, back to the sea. Hardly a day goes by now when I can go out without wellies; I light the fire every evening and watch the flames while the air whirls round the house and whistles in the chimney. And this month gives me space, longer evenings, more quiet times as nights grow longer. The season may be slightly longer in this garden because the mountain shelters it from the north east wind, that demon which comes from the snows of Siberia, whipping icy blasts along the rocky ribs of Wales.

Walking down by the river one day, searching for the lost goose, I looked back at the house and could see how cleverly the site had been chosen. Tucked well back into the hillside, it looks out at the sun all day from a moon-shaped arc of protecting outcrops, with trees to the west and high hills behind. Frost slides down the slope and usually avoids the front garden. On cold winter mornings I have seen the white curve of frost across the meadow and the sheep sheltering above it by the garden hedge. No doubt the stone buildings also help to retain the daytime heat from the sun. geraniums in the big butter crock by the back door have survived some very hard frosts while those in shade by the front door usually die. There must be warmer spots in every garden, particularly close to sunny walls.

Weather permitting, there is always something left to be done outside. This year I managed to clear the buttercups and ground elder from the long flower bed, dividing and replanting daisies, lupins, geraniums, poppies and other perennials just before the frost arrived. I was given a delphinium, something I had always wanted but never managed to grow. This time I have hopes it may survive because the ducks have eaten most of the slugs and snails that used to devour the young shoots.

This is the month to think about ordering roses so they can be sent bare rooted and planted while they are dormant. They do better than wrapped plants or the potted ones from garden centres. I have found that wrapped ones, their roots painted with green wax, take three years to flower, if they survive at all, whereas those dug up and posted at the right time grow so vigorously they flower in their first summer. I can spend hours looking at rose catalogues, writing down their names, deciding what I would like to plant, what might like to grow here and then what I can afford. However, a word of warning about ordering plants by post; special offers of colourful collections, illustrated so temptingly, too often turn out to be tiny, wilted roots which have travelled too far and been uprooted too soon from such rich growing mixtures that they may not survive at all in ordinary garden soil. The lesson is – buy by post only from reputable growers.

That first November I had spent a watery weekend searching for the original land drains and rodding them out. While doing so I discovered the remains of an old well. There is something incredibly exciting about striking water and unblocking old water courses. Most people seem to enjoy it, whatever their age. The process of working with whatever exists is a way of living it has taken me all my life to arrive at. Now I want to say to the young 'Trust your own perception; do not waste time and energy trying to fulfil other peoples' expectations of you; develop what is already there, who you are, what you can do and be, and trust the growing process, with all its seasons and changes.' Like trees, we are all different; a willow cannot be an oak, but everyone has the potential to be something special. Education is increasingly to do with explanations and definitions; the everyday material world is not simple and survival requires considerable concentration on complicated information. But, if our growth gets stunted and we ignore what is going on, we store up problems.

When the clocks change in the autumn there is more time to read and think during the evenings, or in bed on dark mornings, more excuses to not go out of the gate, more inclination to write and hardly any opportunities for gardening. After my visit to Chartres I decided to make a maze in the garden. I had travelled by devious, spiralling ways, with several false starts and dead ends, before I reached this place, so it seemed appropriate – and it might intrigue the children.

I remember slogging uphill in the desolate, dry landscape of Ladakh and wondering why I was doing it; then, reaching a pass at over 17,000 feet, gasping for breath and dazed by the sight of so much land and sky beneath me, I knew. I descended in a dream, legs swinging free like an uncontrolled marionette, to collapse under a tree by a stream, then on again to the cool gloom of a gompa in a tiny green oasis village surrounded by colossal peaks and eroded, rainbow coloured rock. The curious children must have also wondered what I was doing, but the monks probably knew.

The experience of independence, hardship and wilderness, with all its contrasts and shocks, was a private pilgrimage, undertaken when responsibilities became less pressing, which enlarged my view of the world and changed me. To embark on such a journey to some holy place was a traditional, middle aged activity in the east. In the west more people do it when they are young. When I finally set out I found it hard to come back, but eventually I realised that the outward momentum was changing to an inner growth which could continue quietly at home.

When I was small I did not want to grow up and join the world outside, but I did like the idea of becoming an old woman sitting in a garden with a shady hat and rings on her fingers, like my grandmother. Later I wished I could be a poet, but that seemed unlikely since I thought such people were men with long, white beards, like God. My adolescent ambition was to be the first woman on the summit of Everest; that had to be abandoned too, but not before I had seen it. While trying, unwillingly, to grow up I began to notice that women rarely managed anything much by themselves, so I thought the answer might be to marry a poet who climbed mountains. I did not do that either. I had so little idea of what it might mean to be an adult that the reality was an interesting shock. The process is more gradual these days, although everything else changes more quickly. By underestimating what was possible I suppose I let myself be guided by instinct and did not let go of my dreams. I found the rings in the Himalayas and my fingers have thickened so much I shall never take them off, but I am still looking for the right hat.

'Old mother, give me of thy wood;
and I shall give some of mine
when I am turned into a tree.'

Traditional spell.

Chapter 8
DECEMBER

Of the season of goodwill, DARKNESS and the Winter Solstice.

'This is the time of tension between dying and birth
The place of solitude where three dreams cross between
blue rocks.
But when the voices shaken from the yew tree drift away
Let the other yew tree be shaken and reply,
Blessed sister, holy mother, spirit of the fountain, spirit of
the garden
Suffer us not to mock ourselves with falsehood
Teach us to care and not to care
Teach us to sit still...'

T.S. Eliot – 'Ash Wednesday' – V1

At this time of year my inclinations are to curl up like a mouse or bulb and stay somewhere warm and snug, with as little interruption as possible. There

are books to be read; words to be found in unopened
notebooks; photographs to be stuck in albums; letters to
be written; things to be made, mended, cleared out and
tidied up indoors, until the year turns me into a gardener
again. But, as it is, the merry season fast approaches and
so there will only be a few weeks to play with.

Someone suggested on the radio that it was a pity we
did not introduce more colour into our gardens to cheer
us up during the darker months, but I enjoy the contrasts
of the black and white winter world. The trees are magnificent, standing stark and vigorous, their shapely bones
exposed to the wind and wet. You can see the individual
characters of trees better when they are bare, the different ways they grow. Several trees in the wood behind
the house came down in the gales; a tall ash, wreathed
in ivy, a dead sycamore similarly supported and a couple
of spindly pine.

There is some colour left; wet birch branches turn
purple and crimson in the light of an afternoon sunset;
gorse is in flower next to a holly which has retained its
berries – the birds have already stripped most of them.
But it is not colour that transforms this landscape; it is
light. Winter light is so precious and pure. The cold re-
fines it and adds magic sparkle to every pale gleam from
the sun. The air smells so clean on a frosty morning.
Attempting to produce colour at this time of year is a bit
like buying fruit out of season; it dilutes the pleasure of
strawberries in June if you can eat them in December. I
would rather wait and then be overjoyed by spring flowers. Americans maintain that the British are very good
at something called delayed gratification, which means
we were taught early to save the jam in the doughnut
to the end, whereas in the USA apparently they suck it

all out first. However, there is one winter flower which I want to try – the Christmas rose. On a visit to the Lake District one raw December I was introduced to this miraculous flower which opened its rich petals in a bed full of frosted dead leaves, on Christmas morning. Such a flower adds to the real magic of Christmas when we are sometimes threatened by impossibilities, as we struggle to live up to childhood memories of a lighted tree, wood smoke, roasting chestnuts and the choir of Kings' College chapel, and try to hand on the best of these mixed up rituals to the next generation.

I enjoy the Winter Solstice and the idea of saving up sunshine in an evergreen tree; I feel sympathy with the fundamental symbolism of a secret birth at the darkest time of the year; I love the Christian Christmas story, but the approach of this festival feels like a relentless tidal wave that is sure to engulf me in a surfeit of everything. I am not ready for it, yet; I want to hibernate for a while first and work up the energy for it. Every year I see mothers and grandmothers, school teachers and children, dropping like ninepins from colds and flu, followed by too many meals, drinks and late nights, exposure to foreign germs, family stress, long journeys and cold weather. We want to be together; we want to be happy. I want it to work. This year I think I may have cracked it, although the system needs to be tested on a house full of children. I did manage to hibernate for three weeks at the beginning of December. I revelled in the short, dark days; drew the curtains at three o'clock with glee, shut the doors and settled down to slow, silent, solitary evenings and ritualistic occupations. One evening there was a power cut from five o'clock until after midnight. This gave me real taste of darkness, solitary darkness. When I tried to read by candlelight I discovered one candle is not enough. I found it difficult to wrap up presents; I certainly could not sew, so I had a long, hot bath, lit the fire and gazed at it through a glass of mulled elderberry wine. The next day I decided to make a six candle candlestick out of papier mâché and light it on the festival of San Lucia, just before Christmas, as a new way of celebrating the movement from darkness into light. I made other things out of newspaper and wall paper paste as presents and decorated them with intricate, repetitive patterns of dots, lines or stylized animals inspired by aboriginal paintings. This proved to be a very soothing, meditative activity – a wonderful antidote to pre-Christmas panic. After that I was able to plunge into the card writing, carol singing, cooking and sociability with real enthusiasm, and even managed to polish the silver gravy boat.

Little things help a lot. I heard of a new kind of stuffing which does not entail scratching chestnut skins with your fingernails in the middle of the night; I cut a few boughs of holly early, before the birds eat all the berries, and kept them in water instead of tucked behind pictures where they dry up and shed berries on the floor. Cards can be pushed between books, where they are legible the right way up and easier to put up, instead of hanging them on strings from the ceiling by balancing on a chair and twisting your neck. I also sent less cards, and received less, so I imagine everyone was as relieved as I was. I bought what had to be bought in local shops before the rush set in, but I did not start before the season settled on us like one grandmother I met who had the whole thing under her belt by the end of the summer holidays. In the end the domestic tidal wave never

arrived, I relaxed and enjoyed it all. Next year I must
remember to allow myself enough darkness before the
lighting of the lamps.

* * *

At last I caught the gander. After three week with
swans, living on water weed, he was very hungry and
trying to get home, but could not fly uphill. This time
I managed to cut him off from the river and chase him
into the pine copse, which is thick and almost impenetrable. I saw him hide behind a stump of bog oak so
I was able to creep in on my hands and knees, unseen.
Then, gathering determination and strength, I pounced,
grabbing him firmly by the neck with one hand. His
frantic struggles had me flat on my back, wings beating
over me, feet scrabbling at my thighs, wide open beak
hissing in my face. This must have looked, if it had been
visible from anywhere, much like the legendary congress
of Leda and the swan, a vision that did flash through
my mind as I hung on desperately to the snaking neck.
I managed to get onto all fours again and grab the legs
with my left hand, forcing the poor bird under my right
arm so that I could hold down the beating wings with
an elbow and crawl out of the prickly wood. Once I
could stand up he stopped struggling, but I still had to
negotiate a barbed wire fence and two gates, plod a few
hundred yards uphill and cut the wing feathers before
I could drop the bird into the pen. He received a noisy
welcome from the other geese, but looked as exhausted
as I was. He still has a kink in his neck, poor thing.
     Gales brought down the madam alfred carriere rose
and part of the pergola. After five years of rampant

growth it needed pruning anyway, so I cut back the side
shoots and removed all the dead and straggly bits. Se-
curely tied up again it should produce a mass of fragrant
white blooms next year.

I enjoy the dark days but, as I do the same things each
evening, shut up the birds, feed the cat, draw the curtains, put the kettle on, I notice how quickly these short
days go by, how fast the months, the years. This is what
old age will be, the gradual speeding up of time as it
runs out. Sometimes I wake at night and feel afraid, not
so much of dying, but of running out of time. This is
odd, when time is no longer the enemy it used to be, and
nor is death the ogre it was ten years ago. I revel in a
slower pace of living, enjoy every minute of time that is
my own, of the seasonal processes of making a garden,
writing a book without a deadline, letting things take
their course instead of trying to push myself and everybody else. It is no longer a matter of getting things done,
more of simply doing them. It is a great relief not to be
in a hurry any more. I am comfortable with the idea that
if something cannot be done today it can be done next
month, or next year; that the right opportunity will present itself. I trust the process, whereas I used to rush into
things as soon as I thought of them, frantically working
against time as if there were no tomorrow. Strangely,
now that tomorrow is less certain I have more faith in it.
Yet I still worry in the small hours. The grandchildren
grow up so quickly, have I missed opportunities to get to
know them while they are still fresh and curious, share
things with them at the right moment? Some things I
am already to old to do; what might I have left undone
five years from now? One sleepless night I found myself planning to go to Rumania and look after children

with Aids because soon I would be too old to do it. In
the morning I wondered if that was a valid motive for
undertaking such a task, and if I might not be more useful here. It is not as if there is ever a shortage of things
to do, but perhaps I owe the outside world a bit more
attention.

At Christmas time the begging letters arrive in heaps
and all the starving children of the world cry out to us
for help. It is also the time when the travel brochures begin to fall through the letter box. I spent another a sleepless night wondering if I was too old to reach Mount
Kailas. This is an almost inaccessible place of pilgrimage – the mythical Mount Meru of oriental cosmology, a
mountain of magical beauty high in the western Himalayas, the source of the four sacred rivers, the Ganges,
the Sutlej, the Brahmaputra and the Indus. I nearly set
out to get there once, a final journey, and then decided
it was not necessary; there was plenty to discover in my
own land and further to go, without moving. I had done
enough seeking in distant places and it was time to find
the strength to stay at home. I believe this to be true, but
sometimes, awake at full moon maybe, Kailas beckons
again. Now it is possible to approach it from the south;
now I realise I am too old for it, unless I were prepared
to die in the attempt, as a pilgrim should be. But I am
not going to risk that yet.

At this turning point in the year the sight of the sun
rising and setting becomes more important. The ancient
rituals of propitiation make sense when the sun's repeated disappearances are so apparent. The pagan worship
of sun, moon and stars, rivers and springs, trees and
stones survived Christian attempts to stamp it out. As
the personified gods and goddesses that had grown out

of the old beliefs disappeared, the feelings for them were transferred to a more general reverence for the natural world. J.A McCulloch, writing in 1911 about the religion of the Celts, says, '... ancient nature worship, dowered with immortal youth... bowed low before the blast in patient, deep disdain to rise again in vigour. Preachers, councils, laws inveighed against it, but the old rites continued to be practiced, or survived under a Christian dress and colouring. They are to be found in Breton villages, in Highland glens, in Welsh and Cornish valleys, in Irish townships, and only the spread of school board education with its materialism and uninviting common sense is forcing them at last to yield.' How would he see us now, after two world wars and a technological revolution? Even in these Celtic lands, for most people except farmers, all meaningful connections with the elements and the seasons disappear as we insulate ourselves against them. In a modern city it is quite hard to guess what time of day it is, let alone what time of year.

December 21 – the Winter Solstice.

The valley is a sheet of water. So much rain has fallen out of the sky and streamed down the mountain the dykes cannot cope. The floods increase every day. Trees grow out of islands and, each morning, I gaze out over a larger shining lake where swans feed and seagulls gather. The ducks are in heaven, puddling all over the flooded lawn. I have had to lower the dam to let the water out of the pond and reduce the level. Too long under water cannot be good for shrubs, although the irises and primulas seem to like it. Today I waited for the sun to rise so I could mark the place where it comes over the mountain on the shortest day and record it by planting a stone in the perimeter of the maze. The sun's complete arc is just visible at midwinter from this point in the garden. While I was waiting to confirm this satisfying state of affairs, I collected two barrow loads of cow dung from around the standing stone beyond the gate. This is where the cattle sheltered during the gales last month so there was plenty of it. Mixed with water and left for three months this will make excellent plant feed. I had calculated, with the compass, that the sun should appear in the waterfall cleft between the two hills to the south east at half past nine. And it did. This is the first time I have seen it for over a week. The morning is crisp and bright, with snow on the hills and some of the flood water has frozen. I walked down to watch the gulls and swans feeding where sheep usually graze. The valley looks so beautiful under water; this is how it must have looked hundreds of years ago, before it was drained. I wish it could stay like this, but soon the pasture will be needed for the new lambs. At noon the shadow of the tree at the centre of the maze falls on the stone. As the sun drops through the short afternoon the air gets colder and ice forms in straight lines across the flood water, branching like a tree as it spreads out, with jagged, crystalline edges. The sun sets behind the Beacon Hill at half past three. After dark the moon rises so high it is reflected in the pond, as it was in May, but this time it is dashing between dark clouds and wearing a coloured halo, a ring of rainbow ice crystals. The cat rubs against my ankles; the lighted window of the house looks warm and inviting. I bring the Christmas tree indoors – a fir tree, one of the trees dedicated to the

Winter Solstice in the Celtic Tree Calender; the other is yew. Both signify vowels in the tree alphabet — A and I. The symbolic colour of the yew is white, of the fir pied black and white, most appropriate for this time of darkness and light.

Everything is prepared now; I am ready for Christmas.

Chapter 9
JANUARY

Of TREES, the maze, ritual and a place to sit.

> '... as I age in the world it will
> rise and spread, and be for this
> place horizon and orison, the
> voice of its winds. I have made
> myself a dream to dream of
> its rising, that has gentled my
> nights...'

'Planting Trees' – Wendell Berry.

January 12.
I can feel the days getting longer already. The ducks and geese are going in half an hour later and I am waking an hour earlier. Today is new moon – a silver face looking left instead of right. The year is like that – there are no gaps in its progression – as soon as the last rose petal has fallen daffodils push through the cold, wet earth. In parts of Africa where

the weather is always warm, the seasons are continu-
ous and flowers and fruit appear in an unbroken cycle
of growth. Here they lie dormant when conditions
are not conducive to growth, but not for long. Once
the days begin to grow longer, plants stir, even if we
don't. Today the sun came out and I spent an hour or
two pulling out brambles from the upper bank, with
intervals for gazing at the view. The valley is still a
lake, sparkling with light. Two new-born calves are
standing with their mothers beside the standing stone;
there are rams with the sheep in the meadow and the
ducks' new feathers gleam green and purple in the
sunshine.

Some days are like that, but winter was far from over. On fine days I visited my trees. After five years those tiny wild seedlings I carried home in my pocket from many a walk begin to look like the trees they will become; they are part of the future, a time that will contain my grandchildren but not me. So I treat them with respect and shape them thoughtfully. Visiting trees is a great pleasure; I enjoy deciding how to prune them. As they grow they develop personalities, as we do, dependent upon the circumstances of their infancy and youth. Some grow straight, others develop kinks and contortions. The cat climbed the willow by the spring when they were both young and the tree now has an interesting 'S' bend at eye level where the leading shoot was bent over too often. I put a splint on it at one stage and the splint has become part of the tree. Now it has matured these aberrations are no longer a fault; they give the tree its character, and 'S' stands for Saille, the old Irish word for willow.

Someone once asked me to imagine myself as I would like to be twenty years on. I immediately saw myself standing in this garden among tall trees. There were no trees when I came but now there are. Planting trees gives you a place in the future, as children and grand children do. I nurtured those tiny saplings through wind and drought, surrounding them with rings of plastic or roofing felt to protect them from the summer jungle; I provided them with bottles of water to drip into their roots when I went away; trimmed off the lower twigs; gave them support against gales, tying them with old tights to protect the young bark from abrasion. So trees can feel like your children, as John Fuller's did:

'Living a good way up a mountain
Above the natural line of trees
We nurture saplings, ache for torn
Or wounded cedar, oak or thorn
And mourn fatalities.'

Eventually it will be the trees that give the garden its shape, its dimensions and depth, but it will take a year or so and, meanwhile, we have to imagine how it will be. I am aiming at an evergreen backdrop for bulbs, under birch and ash, in the bowl at the back. These dark depth will contain the evergreen oak, a yew tree which will be young long after my children are dead and buried, an arbutus, a romantic tree which produces red strawberries and white flowers at the same time, with rhododendrons and a few pines. It was while gazing down at this from a bench on the path above that I noticed the accidental circle of ash saplings which will contain the maze. At first I thought I would mow it and build a seat round the

central tree but then I realised it was the perfect place
for a maze. One fine morning in the new year, when the
moon and my energy were waxing, I began to clear the
turf from this circle of trees and level it. I tied a piece
of string to the central tree and stretched it as far as the
next one and moved it round. It touched the other trees
exactly. Then I also discovered that these trees marked
the directions of the midsummer and midwinter sun-
rises and the midwinter sunset. This little bit of luck
confirmed the notion that the maze might have a double
role.

The idea of a maze or labyrinth is very ancient and
appears in many cultures all over the world. Perhaps
the first maze was a spiral drawn with a finger in the
sand, an unself-conscious doodle. Simple spirals appear
on Neolihic tombs like new Grange, in Ireland, where
the sun reaches a triple spiral carved on the interior
wall for a few minutes at the midwinter sunrise. There
are similar devices in the rock temples of Mexico. The
famous Minoan temple at Knossos, with the legendary
labyrinth which housed the Minotaur, was supposed to
have existed before the fall of Crete in 1500 BC. Early
classical mazes were single, meandering pathways leading to the centre by devious means, depicted sometimes
on coins or pots related to temple dancers. There were
no choices in these mazes The same motif was used by
the Romans in mosaics and by the great cathedral builders of medieval Europe. In Britain they were also made
by monks, who walked them as a spiritual practice, but
their pagan flavour continued. They were often cut
into turf on the hillside where younger members of the
community would disport themselves on May Day. The
original connection with Troy remained in the common

name for turf mazes. Later mazes were designed with blocked ways and diversions which led you astray; you were supposed to get lost in them. They became fashionable puzzles in gardens, planted with tall hedges, including statues and hidden seats where couples could spend a diverting hour or two, well concealed. Some designs became complex mathematical puzzles, decorative, like Elizabethan knot gardens which were arrangements of dwarf hedges, flowers and herbs. In recent years the tradition has returned to the garden. Maze designers have devised new ones or rescued old ones, so that today there are over a hundred mazes open to the public in Britain, and many more being grown in private – hidden labyrinths waiting to be walked in secret gardens.

My maze will be a classical labyrinth with seven windings, made out of white quartz pebbles. A method for drawing a maze has been passed on, with variations, throughout history. You begin by making a cross, as if within a square; then you place a dot in each corner of the imaginary square; you take a line from the top left dot, up and around the outside if the dot top right, then down to join the top of the cross. The next line starts at the top right dot, circles up and over the top of the cross and then below the top left dot and continues up and around the top in a circle until it meets the right hand end of the cross. The next line begins at the bottom left dot, goes up to the left in a wider circle right around the circle outside the bottom right dot and back inside itself, up and around to meet the left end of the cross. Finally, start at the remaining, unattached bottom right dot and take the line around the circle between the two lines to circle inside the bottom left dot at the end of the last line and then go up and around the circle, outside everything,

HOW TO DRAW A MAZE

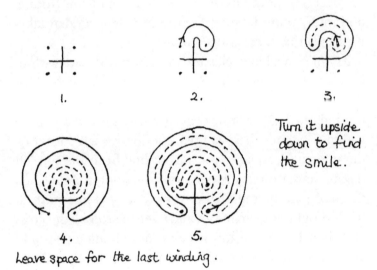

1.

2.

3.

Turn it upside
down to find
the smile.

4.

5.

Leave space for the last winding.

to reach the bottom of the cross. This is quite hard to do without the diagram.

Another idea had been incubating during the winter. The bowl, or cauldron shape of the back garden is a cosy hollow from which stone was quarried to build the barns. It is sheltered and private – a good site for a seat. There is a feeling of being between two worlds, at the entrance to somewhere else. I realised that what I was hoping to build would be a kind of lap, a comfortable enclosed shape you could curl up in and look out at the space between the hills.

In Welsh legends Ceridwen's cauldron contained the brew which gave re-birth to the bard Taliesin, whose magical claims are woven into the matter of Wales.

'Before men walked
I was in these places
I was here
When the mountains were laid
I looked up
At the making of stars
I stand erect
At the birth of rivers
Observed
The designing of flowers'

I imagined an abstracted female form, with boulder like head, shoulders and knees and a comfortable space to sit between them. I remember watching children clambering over a massive bronze figures by Henry Moore beside the Serpentine; how they placed themselves, settled in and became part of the sculpture. When nervous officials asked the sculptor if he minded he had replied.'

We wore hobnailed boots when I was a boy; now they don't.' He was pleased to see small children so at home in his massive laps, sliding down those huge smooth knees.

I would have to continue the theme of re-cycled materials – an old chair, rubble, wire netting, river boulders. Moving enough material to makes these shapes would be hard work; I would have to wait until the ground was drier. Meanwhile I made a few clay maquettes and thought about it. Perhaps parts of the lady could be made of turf; I could clip her hair, grow trailing plants over her knees and fragrant herbs in her elbows.

The garden began with the finding of the spring, the clearing out of the stream and the panting of trees, It continues with colour and places to go, with producing food and nurturing people. I hope this central feature – the maze, the sundial and the lap – hidden in the wildest part of the garden will help to join everything together. The lap will be a special place to sit, the maze something else for children to do. For me both are to do with the ending of one spiralling journey and the beginning of another – ending at the beginning and beginning at the end.

* * *

One day, after the valley had been flooded for over two months, the national Rivers Authority arrived in force. Cars and vans parked in the road; Land Rovers and lorries churned up the verges and diggers trundled along the river banks to reach the flooded dykes. Two divers tried to clear the huge pipe which takes the water from one side of the valley to the other, under the river, but they could not use a chain saw under water to clear the debris blocking the pipe. It took a week to pump the water out and another before the fields dried out. Then the water meadows looked a bit like a Christmas pudding, dark and blotchy with rushes and mud under the low white cloud draping the mountains. I missed the lake.

In the Celtic Tree Calender January is related to the duck. Towards the end of this month they begin to disport themselves, showing off their glorious purple and emerald plumage, dipping and diving and chasing each other round and round. Such seasonal connections made practical sense when they were made. We create structures to make sense of our world.

Living, as I do now, a fairly solitary existence in which animals, growing things, seasons, elements and the movements of heavenly bodies feature prominently, I am continuously surprised by the satisfaction these basic circumstances provide. I am also aware that one of the ingredients in this magic mix is time, lots of it. If I were a farmer working twelve hours a day to make my living from the land I might not feel the same about it. Modern life provides few rituals of any psychological or spiritual significance. We usually ignore the natural rhythms of our bodies and the seasons and then invent complicated and expensive substitutes for things we no longer have time for. An exercise machine cannot be compared with a walk in the hills. However, we can still create private rituals even if public ones have been mislaid by our culture. It is not self indulgent to lie under a tree instead of shopping; it is sane and it's free.

The rhythms of garden and animals need no more explanations. My rituals might. They are essentially private; I acknowledge the moon and fit my activities to the energy levels it seems to affect. I star gaze, particularly at Venus, the first to appear and the last to fade – being aware of the distance between ourselves and the stars is comforting; it puts things into perspective. Sunrise and sunset are easy to celebrate. Thunder storms are a release from tension; rainbows are marvels which often span the valley when the hills are purple under cloud and the pastures as bright as burnished brass. A walk in the wind and the rain blows away niggling worries, rattling windows are reassuring when I am warm in bed.

January

Today I pruned 'New Dawn'; she was getting very straggly and falling off the wall. I found some snowdrops coming out under the log. The butterfly hibernating on the kitchen window sill is opening its wings – a tortoiseshell. The wild plums are full of yellow hammers, glowing like small fruits on dead twigs. The red kite circled over the wood until the buzzards chased it away. The garden is a bog, but I managed to move seven barrow loads of rocks from various places, one or two at a time, to make a curb around the maze. New shoots are appearing on most of the roses but I resist pruning them in case they die back in the frost. But I have pruned the apple trees, removing unwanted branches and shortening others, and given the willow its winter haircut. I stuck several bits of it into the circle that will become a willow house where some of last year's cuttings died. I moved two loads of rubble to the 'Lap', but the ground is too wet to do more now.

Chapter 10
FEBRUARY

Of ENERGY, Zen stones and serendipity.

'Retire when the work is done
This is the way to Heaven.'

Tao teaching by Lao Tsu – 6th century BC.

February.
I sit at the bedroom window, looking out across the valley. The sun is shining and there are lambs in the meadow, but it is still very cold outside and I feel no inclination to go out and do anything yet. February is the 2 o'clock in the morning of the year when energy levels are very low, and this week is the dark phase of the moon. I am learning to to be patient and to rest at these times, to trust that energy will return when it is needed. But the garden is responding to longer days and beginning to show signs of life. Daffodils are coming up and so are the crocuses I planted in October. Last year the voles ate them; this time I dug

deeper holes. There are mole hills everywhere except the front lawn; the moles must have heard me say I might set traps if they crossed it. At the back they have excavated a network of tunnels and these have become underground streams which cave in when I tread on them. It rained again in the night, so everything sparkles. A small wind is feathering the surface of the pool, shaking the spiky reflections of irises. Birds sing as if spring had arrived, but this is deceptive. The wind is from the north east and brings flurries of snow. I feel sorry for flowers triggered by increasing hours of daylight; they will get such a battering during the next few weeks.

I wish I was feeling stronger. The edges of the pond need attention since floods, frost, ducks and children have taken their toll and the cement has cracked away from the paving stones. But primroses and primulas have survived the inundations. Outside the kitchen window snowdrops shine against the dark rocks of the waterfall; I planted them there to be visible from indoors on days like this and I want masses more of them; they are such perfect, heartwarming flowers. I remember how my father loved them. His birthday was in February and he died in the same month; so did my mother, at the lowest hour. I remember the frozen furrows in the field outside her window and the seagulls screaming above as the last rays of the winter sun gilded their breast feathers. Perhaps I will sink with the season, the sun and the moon when it's my turn. These night thoughts have disturbed my sleep, but the snowdrops are there when I wake in the morning.

The best way to get snowdrops to grow is to uproot them and transplant them from somewhere else while they are still flowering – new bulbs rarely come up. I hope to fill the garden with bulbs before I die, like trees, they go on and on, flowering faithfully year after year, increasing without any attention. You can never have too many of them because they retire gracefully when their performance is completed, leaving room for the next act – a good example to us all. When the stalwart Daffs' reappear under the hedge to withstand the spring gales, I wonder about the farmer's wife who planted them there – how many generations ago? What would she think of the place now? So much has changed.

Those daffodils, a red currant bush, the sweet smelling broom and the rambling roses were the only things in the garden when I arrived. After all the manual labour of that first dry winter, wind and wet in February gave me a chance to take stock. While I was planning what to plant where those daffodils, tall and tough, forced their way through the jungle of thorn and couch grass along the boundary hedge and proved their permanence. I have always loved daffodils. When I was seventeen, climbing in Snowdonia and discovering mountains for the first time, then tearfully tearing myself away to return to flat Suffolk and become an art student, I remember vowing to plant daffodils on the triangle of grass outside Pen y Gwryd in memory of those happy days. It would probably be too high up there, but all along the verges of new motorways, and some minor roads, thousands of daffodils appear every spring as a celebration everyone can share – a tribute to the imagination of those who planted them. What better way to lift the spirit after a long winter and welcome visitors to Wales?

During those first two years of living in Wales my energy, born of the excitement of continuous creation in
this consummate setting, did not let me down as long
as I paced myself and did not do things in a hurry. If
I overdid it, my back gave out, so it was worth taking
care. I learned these lessons the hard way. It is impa-
tience, bad temper, frustration or self-induced panic that
upsets the balance and causes accidents. I was suffering
from all that and running down some steps when I fell
and twisted an ankle. I had to keep it up for a few days,
wrapped in packets of frozen peas. When I know I have
over-used my back I hang from the stairs by my arms for
a minute, stretching the lumbar region, and this usually
obviates a visit to the osteopath. Lifting boxes of food
from the back of the car, hoovering and bed making are
best avoided for a while. Hoeing is fatal so I never use
one now. To lift without hurting the back I learned to
make a triangle with knees and arms and take the strain
with the legs and never lift and twist together. Tall people need these techniques as they get older, and learning to take frequent short rests and change the activity
becomes more important. I am lucky to have a very old,
long bath to stretch out in at the end of the day.

Once the terraces, walls and paths were established
and the general shape of the garden was becoming
clear, one thing led to another, and another. The process
was continuous but, when the weather was bad or I was
waiting for energy to return, I would recollect all the
activities
    and ideas that were going into the making of a new
garden and record them. I sometimes wonder what will
happen to this garden when I'm gone. The shrubs and
trees will grow bigger; water and stone will keep their

shape; smells will remain even if the place returns to
the wilderness it was when I found it. The daffodils will
re-appear every spring as they have since the farmer's
wife first planted them. It would still be a lovely place
to inherit and care for, but somebody might hack it all
down and start again.

When the ponds were first dug the earth that came
out of them went to other parts of the garden. In such
a rocky situation top soil, which takes years to make, is
always wanted somewhere. It made homes for climbing
roses, honeysuckle and clematis in retaining walls against
buildings where rock was only a few inches below the
surface; it deepened vegetable plots and flower beds. I
levelled some places and built up banks with turf turned
upside down. Huge heaps of weeds left rotting on concrete in the yard turned into soil within two years, as did
piles of turf stripped from rock. I made raised vegetable
plots, each one no more than six foot square, deeply dug
and edged with old planks or beams. I try not to walk
on them and stand on a board to weed and sow. If the
soil remains loose it is easier to deal with and plants can
grow closer together and root more deeply, leaving less
room for weeds. Ideally these deep beds should be built
up every year with more compost and manure. This is
how vegetables were grown hundreds of years ago in
France. The night soil collected in Paris was taken to the
outskirts of the city and dumped on small plots of land,
layered with straw and left to rot down. Superb vegetables grown on these rich heaps were picked each morning and carried back to city markets on the same carts.

The materials I used for many construction projects
were things I found lying about. Farmyards and old
barns usually accumulate such things – posts, beams, old

shafts and bits of rusted iron machinery. I found slate slabs and broken bricks in the foundation of a demolished shed two feet underground; I rolled and levered rocks and found them new places to settle. Some giant boulders were released when two windows were made into doorways; they were so big I despaired of moving them alone, but was too impatient to wait for help. I knew where I wanted them to go and was determined to get them there. One particular rock was sitting outside the kitchen door. I wanted to use it as part of a future barbecue site and this meant rolling it a yard or so closer to the wall of the house. I put my back against it with my hands underneath, as if pushing a car, and heaved. Nothing happened. I fetched a crow bar and tried to lever it up a bit; the crow bar sank in nicely but nothing happened to the boulder. I left it and returned to building a retaining wall round the herb garden with smaller rocks. But all that morning the big one sat there, confronting me. At lunch time I tried again, without success. Perhaps I needed a rest. I sat in the sun eating bread and cheese and looking at it. I drank a glass of beer and thought about it. How did they build Stonehenge, this house, these barns? How did they get those massive rocks up so high? The next door barn has only nine courses from the ground to the gable and, although they talk about horses and pulleys, no one has been able to explain exactly what they did, except that most of the building work was done after a full days work on the land, some of it unpaid.

After lunch I went in search of suitable larger levers and planks. The good things about owning a barn is that I never need to throw anything useful away and I never say no to other people's junk. When I am starting a job it is what I find that helps me decide what to do or how to do it. This is one of the principals of serendipity, (defined in the O.D. as the faculty of making happy and unexpected discoveries by accident.) So I returned to the rock with several logs of wood, a broken oar, two breeze blocks, some bricks, two halves of stout scaffolding plank and a few bits of metal piping. It is not easy to describe exactly what I did with these items of equipment; as far as I remember I did a number of different things, using them in various combinations, with intervals to consider the effects, which were minimal. Then I decided I was making a complete fool of myself. After all, I was a lone granny with a bad back; what on earth made me think I could move a rock of such dimensions? It was an utter waste of time and energy; no one else would be so stupid. So I downed tools and stomped off to do some other garden task.

It was a long summer day. I suppose I returned to the boulder about five times. At last I really gave in. There was no way I was ever going to move it. I would ask someone else to do it for me – a much more graceful thing to do anyway. I had completely let go of the arrogant idea of doing it myself and went indoors to have a bath.

Later, listening to my favourite outdoor Mozart and watching the light change on the mountain, with my feet up and a drink in my hand, the rock looked different, smaller. I do not remember thinking about it; I just got up and wandered past it, giving the bricks underneath a shove with my foot. Just for fun I picked up the crow bar and slid it under the plank from a slightly different angle. The end stuck against something hard in a comforting kind of way, so I gave it an experimental wrench. The rock moved. It slid about an inch along the plank. I did it again; it slid again, almost rolled, slipped sideways and re-settled about two feet further on. I pushed everything back underneath it and repeated the process until the rock was exactly where I wanted it to be.

Since that day I have continued to believe in miracles. Was that how they built Stonehenge, Carnac and Avebury, little by little, undisturbed by notions of time, self doubt or fear of failure, trustfully enabling the weight of the rocks and the elements to help them? Or did they force gangs of terrified slaves to implement their ambitious dreams? In the martial arts the energy of the attack is turned skilfully back upon the attacker, so the faster he comes, the harder he falls. Although I learned a lot from this boulder episode, in my case no skill was employed; it was simply a happy accident which was able to take place once I had let go the idea of making it happen.

Serendipity is something I have come to value more and more. It means that, when I plan to make something – an arch, a fence, gate, chicken coop, cold frame or whatever it may be – a visit to the barn will probably produce JUST enough wood to do it, in suitable lengths, more or less. The search for nails and screws will also discover JUST enough of the right sizes. I enjoy doing things this way because I have to be inventive. I know I am not in control altogether, nor am I having to follow instructions, which I dislike because they seem to sap my confidence, enthusiasm and ingenuity. I prefer to invent ways of doing things even if it means making mistakes which have to be corrected. The little strokes of luck are always encouraging. If, on the other hand, things keep going wrong, it probably means that the idea has not been thought through, it was the wrong idea or it is being undertaken at the wrong time, or in the wrong way.

The right time for doing a job is the second principle of serendipity. It is absolutely no good, at this stage of life, for me at least, to attempt an ambitious job unless I am in the right mood for it, mentally and physically. In fact, I know now that I have more creative and physical energy when the moon is waxing. Perhaps this was always true, but I was unaware of it. There are always a number of things that need doing; I write them down when I think of them in case I forget what they are when the opportunity for doing them arrives. Then I do the job that grabs me first. If and when it palls I swap to another. The thing you feel like doing on that day is the one you will do best; the others can probably wait. Different activities require different kinds of energy and energy fluctuates like the weather. It is the first time in my life I have been able to carry out this theory and prove that it works. Nobody is telling me what to do or how to do it. The results serve their purposes and cost almost nothing.

Much of the debilitating stress suffered in the work place is the result of lack of real motivation – 'living a script written by someone else'. Wearing out the worker in the name of efficiency is unproductive in the long term. Most people are creative and want to be active, but not all in the same way. Since hours of daylight change throughout the year; maybe we would do better if we took lessons from the birds and spread our workloads more unevenly, adjusting the artificial regime of nine to five according to the season, not only on the land.

* * *

When the ponds first filled with water, I sat on the new
terrace to look at them. It had taken about a week for the
silt to settle but they needed no lining. They looked good.
Their shapes echoed the shapes of the view beyond, the
sweep of hedges and hills, the curves in the surface of
fields, and I could almost believe it was this stream which
became the shining loop of river far below. Although the
scale was so different it did look as if the garden were
part of the landscape. The sound of water falling over
stone was very soothing. By moving the stones about I
had discovered I could produce different kinds of watery sounds. An old fire hose someone had given me,
buried and protected by slates, was bringing the water
from the stream to this hand built waterfall near the
back door; the new stream fed the ponds, one slightly
higher than the other, and the second one overflowed
into the field ditch. Then I began to arrange big stones
and smaller ones around the edges, rolling them in and
out of the water until they looked natural. There was a
small island in the first pond and this arrangement of
stones was inspired by a Zen gardening book from which
I had learned how to pair stones and provide them with
children – two large contrasting stones grouped with a
number of smaller ones, as if they were talking to each
other. I learned many other things too – how to arrange
a view with diminishing horizontal curves so that it is
restful to the moving eye; how to frame it with verticals
that increase perspective, with a focus point on which to
pause and soften the gaze. All this must not look devised
but as if it had happened by itself, as, of course, it often
has. When planning a garden time spent doing nothing
but looking at it is time well spent. It takes time to soak
up what we see and process it. All kinds of things will

happen on their own if we let them, by suspending our urges to subdue and control. We are merely partners in this business.

Once the shapes of the ponds had established themselves I hammered overlapping broken slates into the ground around the edges to strengthen them and planted wild, damp-loving things like ferns, rushes, primroses and irises near the water. More broken slates laid flat over polythene sheet between the pond edges and the lawn gives the mower something to cut against, reduces the need to clip the edges and discourages weeds. In some places I laid big, flat stones and these get cemented in bit by bit, whenever I use the cement mixer.

Playing with earth and stone is as satisfying as playing with water; these are the elemental activities that keep children amused all day on the beach. We may grow out of it, but sometimes we deny ourselves simple pleasures when we create more sophisticated expectations. Watch the fathers in the beach, digging huge sand castles to defy the tide. Mothers are often too tired when the children are small; they simply want to lie and sleep in the sun, like animals do, to restore the energy sapped by babies, but grandmothers have a second chance.

Most human beings, unlike animals, once they are rested and their essential work done, look for other ways of exerting themselves, One of the joys of the third age is that. Released from stricter arrangements and no longer slaves to time, we can, like children, play again. I am doing the same kind of things now as I did as a child. These basic occupations and simple pleasures may be hard to come by in adult life; or they have been devalued as occupations to grow out of, or avoid because the parents worked too hard. But it is interesting that occupations like fishing, boating, gardening, weaving or making pots, which were once a means of survival, have become popular leisure pursuits, called pass times. While the chance to get out of the city for the week end may be beyond the reach of many, or simply boring, a house in the country also becomes a distant dream. Not so a garden. Most people in Britain get the opportunity to have one eventually, however small. Gardening has become a national obsession; more and more people who have no economic links with the land are growing things, as if our instincts still respond to a need for green. Even a window box can be a connection to the cycle of the seasons.

Anyone who has a garden can devise their own ways of building things; of re-using junk for original, useful or decorative purposes. Children do it, left to the own devices without toys or television for a couple of days. An initial leap of confidence may be required to use your own ideas instead of waiting for someone to tell you what to do or how, but practice releases creativity and build confidence. It requires time rather than money, ingenuity rather than expertise and a determination to do things in your own way rather than trying to reach some undefined goal set by someone else. It means trusting your own inclinations and instincts instead of attempting to live up to someone else's standards and expectations. There are no shoulds or should nots in a garden; it is a private place, an individual creation.

The old cottage garden was a good example of this approach. Times were harder then; most gardens had to produce food; pleasure gardens were for the leisured rich. There were no garden centres selling a multitude of garden gadgets; no television programmes to tell

people what they ought to be doing. Every cottage garden and allotment displayed individual ingenuity and
creative serendipity. Old bed frames, wheels, bottomless
buckets, shells and saucepans, broken china and chimney pots – everything was re-used; people made gates
with hinges made from old boots, cunning latches which
closed themselves; fences, hen houses, rabbit hutches,
cold frames, bean poles, brooms, sheds and paths were
made from whatever could be found. The results became
decorative by accident, so that now people actually buy
barrels in which to plant geraniums, or hang cartwheels
on the wall. In Greece I remember seeing old hay rakes
hanging on white washed courtyards entwined with
clematis; oil cans, kettles and milk churns painted white
and filled with marigolds, wooden crates and driftwood
nailed together and painted sky blue as garden furniture
– all more original than the wooden wheelbarrow full of
begonias.

In Nepal villagers throw a big wicker basket over a
mother hen and her chicks at night; in Africa children
are wizards with wire, old tins and bottle tops, turning
them into toys and musical instruments; in rural India,
where everything is used at least twice, they descend on
a picnic site for discarded polythene bags, yoghurt cups
or baked bean cans. In places where money and new
consumer goods are hard to come by, people invent ways
of re-using everything.

I had a war time childhood; I hardly remember anything being bought except food and fuel, and not all of
that. We collected firewood, nuts, mushrooms, blackberries and useful junk from rubbish heaps. We grew vegetables and fruit; clothes were second hand or home made;
we found things to play with, or made them. I suppose I

have simply returned to childhood; I recommend it. In an ideal world there would be less difference between work and play; one is simply the preparation for the other. The acquisition and the use of skills to provide for our basic needs, which is so satisfying, has been diluted and separated, soured like milk. There is still drudgery, interspersed with diversion – frenetic activity and frenetic consumption seems to have become an economic necessity. I have found great satisfaction and freedom by finding my own solutions and making things – in my own time. The third age offers more choices, but time, the great gift this stage of life can bring, passes more quickly and energy begins to run out. We have to adapt ourselves again and again to changing conditions, like a snake shedding its skin. As the Buddha taught, nothing is static, solid, separate, permanent, continuous or defined. However, once we accept that and allow ourselves to change, as things do in the garden, everything seems easier.

Chapter 11
MARCH

Of seasonal activity, VEGETABLES, wilderness and the Spring Equinox.

> 'Nature... is beyond our science and arts because its secret is being, not saying. Its greatest value is that it cannot be reproduced, that this being can be apprehended only by other present being, only by the living senses and consciousness. All experience of it through surrogate and replica, through selected image, gardened word, through other eyes and minds, betrays or banishes reality. This is nature's consolation, or message... it can be known and entered only by each, and in its now; not by you through me, by any you through any me; only by you through yourself, or me through myself.'
>
> From 'The Tree' by John Fowles.

March.
March comes in like a lion, with snow and more

*gales. The garden has never had such a battering;
there may be gaps in it this year, which is ironic
since I spent last autumn removing things which had
grown too big. I should have let the weather do it
for me. Will the flowering shrubs which frame the
view of the hills from the house be able to survive
these freezing winds? I can only wait until all risk
of frost is past, cut them right back to stronger buds,
and hope. The snow lasted a week – the first time
this garden has experienced it. I have lost the tree lupin which was protecting other plants but the cuttings
which I set to replace the dreaded knot weed seem to
have survived. There is holly, two kinds of escallonia, wild plum and rhododendron along the boundary
fence now, with ceanothus, buddlea and eucalyptus
just inside it. I wonder what will come up in the blue
bed I planted in front of all that.*

*Snow was some protection and the daffs look well,
in bud, waiting for a little warmth, like us. It has
been the longest winter for years and there is no chance
of spring while the wind remains in the north east.
There is nothing I can do outside; the ground is too
cold and wet. Pruning would be rash until all risk
of frost is past. The green house has lost some panes
so it would be no good planting anything in it until
I have replaced the broken glass. I twisted my ankle
again, in a puddle this time, and have had to keep
the foot up so I am almost glad the weather is awful.
I hope I will feel more like leaping into action before
March goes out like a lamb.*

And of course I did. Spring eventually woke me up
and, with it came new ideas and energy to carry

them out. This had nothing to do with will power; it is an internal shift. We need rest, as growing things do and, if we resist, something happens to enforce the message, like the twisted ankle. Sometimes we need a number of lessons before we learn this – 'it's secret is being, not saying,' or doing.

I began by pruning all those poor, frost bitten shrubs and roses, trying to make good shapes by cutting back to outward facing, healthy looking buds. There was so much to be burned, it accumulated in heaps all over the place, awaiting a drying wind.

Before the bracken grows up a network of badger tracks are visible between the three sets on the hillside behind the house. I am continually blocking holes where these ancient routes pass under fences, but these animals do not change their ways. As the years go by I make short cuts from place to place like they do, through rough areas, so paths develop. Every path has a purpose. Once established they can be emphasized by seats and treats. Every view is a treat; so is a bird table, a sun dial, a sculpture or a special plant or tree, and a seat is a place to pause and notice things. Smells are treats. How about a mass of lavender, lily of the valley or wild garlic beside it, roses or honeysuckle over it? For sound, a waterfall or wind bells; glass bottles filled with different amounts of water wail woefully in the wind; piano wires sing stretched between the branches of a tree; pieces of slate suspended on cord tinkle like bells in a breeze. A garden is a place to exercise all the senses, to wander and wonder. I like the idea of cryptic sentences or verses written on rocks, mysterious signs carved on tree trunks; initials and pets' graves make history.

Ideas and developments keep the garden going; I

have less motivation for maintenance but if I am creating something new I set to work with more vigour and can clear a patch of jungle in no time. Even grass cutting can become a way of making shapes. To decide where or how big a new flower bed may be you can mow until a suitable shape remains. Another method is to lay a garden hose on the ground in great sweeping curves. The best way to plant bulbs is to throw them down and dig holes where they land.

During the wild March days I reflected on the idea of wilderness. Although many people live in places that are effectively 'a support system in outer space', wilderness still exists and always will, however much we try to tame it. The romantic notion that we might all return to a simpler way of life closer to the natural world may not be practical, but when we preserve wide open, green spaces for our refreshment, we tend to devalue the experience by categorizing things so they are recognizable, regulated and repeatable. John Fowles explains it well when he says, '... the danger, in both art and nature, is that all emphasis is placed on the created, not the creation.'

* * *

The first leaves to come out in the garden are those of the weeping willow. Two years ago I had planted a circle of cuttings from the parent tree and, although their roots were wreathed in ice and gales had flattened them, they were still alive and beginning to look like trees. As they grow the idea is to weave the branches together like an up turned basket to make a living beehive hut. Now the saplings were bigger the circle seemed too small, so I moved some of them while the ground was still a bog and began to level the interior. It was so rocky it could only be done in short bursts but, when it was flat, I laid an old carpet on it to keep the weeds at bay. One day, when the branches have grown into trellised walls and the roof throws a dappled green shade, it will be big enough for the children to sleep in on summer nights. I worked out that, if it takes five years for the branches to meet in the middle, the eldest grandchild will not be too old to play in it and the youngest will be old enough. Shrubs which were growing too close to the enlarged willow house were given new homes; this is a good time for moving things around and planting out rooted cuttings, but they need a bit of compost to get their feet into where the ground is rocky.

In the spring, the year after I made the vegetable plots, I constructed three terraces for soft fruit in the boggy jungle behind the house where cows had once waited to be milked. The first, which was a mass of tall nettles, was growing raspberries, blackcurrants the gooseberries within the year, mulched with bonfire ash, old newspapers and wood shavings. In the second I grew potatoes for the first year. The soil was so thin I put layers of newspaper on top of the rough turf, covered them with a few inches of straw and compost and put the seed potatoes on top of that, covered with more straw and compost. Everything rotted down well and produced a superb crop. It worked so well I did the same thing with the top terrace to avoid the back breaking job of digging out the grass. By next year that material will have rotted down too. The second year was wet and the currants got leaf curl. The book said dig them up, which I was loth to do so soon. So I cut the effected branches right back and the next year they produced huge currants and masses

of healthy leaves to hide the fruit from the birds. Blackbirds are less interested in raspberries, which is lucky
because it is almost impossible to spread heavy netting
single handed and the plastic kind gets hopelessly tangled up in new growth. So I used the remains of the torn
netting to protect young onions and peas and hung old
CDs among the fruit bushes – they twinkle in the sun
and seem to make birds nervous. A good crop provides
enough for both of us, as long as I get there first.

The next job was to mend the greenhouse and clear
it out ready for planting seeds. I collected several sacks
of leaf mold from the wood and this was a useful addition to the seed mixture. I planted lettuces, peas, broad
beans and broccoli; then I turned out the envelopes of
seed collected from last year's flowers – night scented
stock, primulas, sweet peas, marigolds nasturtiums, lupins and honesty, planting them all in seed trays and cov-
ering them with damp newspaper and glass until they
germinated.

The green house is really only a cold frame built on
top of one of the pig sties, high enough to stand up in
and just big enough to take the pots and seed trays. During the winter I keep the geraniums and their cuttings
on a deep window sill in the house so that I remember
to water them. So this is really just an extension of the
kitchen windowsill where I used to grow spring seeds.
It was built from part of a collapsed greenhouse and
old windows; the door is two sheets of clear polythene
overlapped, attached to the roof with battens and held
down by two bricks. This arrangement has, surprisingly,
lasted two seasons. Once the seeds were in and while the
ground was still too wet and cold to plant anything out
of doors, there was time to clean out the chickens and

ducks in the old pig sties. When the winter bedding had been raked out and scattered on the compost heaps I could hose down the concrete floors. Several inches of wood shavings make excellent deep litter and remains dry for months. The poultry manure is a great help in the production of good compost to enrich this stoney soil and after a few years of feeding the vegetable plots have improved a lot.

The growing of vegetables on a small scale is not economic if your consider the time put into it, but, in terms of pleasure and satisfaction, I find it is worth the effort. There is nothing quite like stepping out into your own patch of food on a summer evening when you are feeling hungry and trying to decide what to have for supper, picking a few tasty tit bits and making a meal around them. When visitors come it is one of the best shared pleasures of the garden.

March is the month when I begin to imagine the summer crops; I study last year's plans and decide where to plant what, following a simple rotation system – roots followed by leaves and then seeds – with a sprinkling of lime on the cabbage patch. If you plant the same things in the same plot two years running it encourages diseases, especially potato blight, and depletes the soil. Peas and beans fix the nitrogen for the crops that follow. The next thing is to buy the seed, then to wait for the weather to dictate their burial. It does not pay to plant too soon, when the ground is cold; most things catch up when the days are longer and warmer in April. I no longer try to grow anything that does not thrive here, like carrots, which prefer sand. I stick to the vegetables that I know will succeed. The broad beans and parsnips go in first, then spinach beet, Swiss chard, onion sets and shallots, leaks, potatoes and sugar peas; later on french beans and runner beans. Some peas and beans are started out in pots, but the outdoor crops usually do just as well, as long as the mice don't eat them in the ground – a dowsing in paraffin deters them. Tomatoes and courgettes also begin in pots and are planted out in May, but a wet summer can mean they fail to ripen. Radishes and lettuces can be sown all through spring and summer, but some lettuces do not do very well in stoney soil, the red ones seem to do best here. Asparagus is a luxury vegetable I have tried to grow, but without much success. It takes some years to establish and needs a lot of very careful weeding. However, those luscious green shoots, soaked in melted butter and eaten on a summer evening with fresh bread and a glass of white wine are the taste of heaven, so I keep trying.

It was in the Himalayas that I first saw vegetables grown in squares, on irrigated terraces rather than in rows, and I have grown them like that ever since. I sometimes make plans to irrigate the plots from the stream, but I have not done it yet because it always seem to rain just in time. After seeing those well tended, irrigated gardens I had a vivid dream which has stayed with me. I saw one of those little squares planted with lettuces; each plant was surrounded by a puddle of water which had been led through small irrigation channels from a stream higher up; they were all thriving. The lettuces looked alike, but each one was, of course, slightly different from its neighbours; they were all cared for and growing well. Outside, but close by, was as single gnarled and twisted tree which had grown too big and dried of drought. I woke with an enormous sense of relief and happiness. The dream seemed to represent an important shift – the struggle to be special or different was a dead end and unnecessary. We are as we are, we each have what we need to keep growing.

March 21st – the Equinox – and, as usual, the wind drops for one fine, warm day. In this calm pause the garden begins to look like a garden again. The willow waves long green fingers over the pond; there are patches of colour – primroses, primulas, polyanthus, grape hyacinths and, everywhere, daffodils. As I draw the curtains in the evening I see the pansies in the window boxes in bloom – purple hills beyond the purple flowers. From upstairs I watch the lambs jumping up and down on the meadow bank as the shadows lengthen across an emerald green field. The ditch is like a moat overflowing with water. They say it has been the wettest winter for years, yet only two years ago we were suffering from drought.

Energy is returning, great bursts of it – it was not old age, it was winter.

Then there were more gales and hail storms. The poor plants lost wind burnt and frozen shoots, but it calmed down just in time to go out like a lamb, with the changing of the clocks. The ducks and chickens began to lay again and the goose settled down on a nest full of eggs, the gander on guard. During this warm spell I prepared the vegetable beds and planted the first seeds, working all day until I ached all over.

One evening I sat outside sipping the last of the sloe gin, glowing with satisfaction, watching the light turn pink on the mountain and celebrating another turning point in the procession of the seasons. The larches were

showing green again and the gorse blazing. I was study-
ing my record of vegetable rotation when I suddenly
remembered the day and the time – it was as if I had
heard something. I ran out to the gate and there it was –
the full moon, a huge shiny shilling smiling over the edge
of the hill and, opposite, slipping into the sea, the setting
sun, round and red. I stood still between them, savouring
this rare moment of balance.

I walked round the garden sitting on seats, listening to
the stream among friendly, nodding daffodils, dreamily
drinking it in – spring. I planted out more cuttings – honeysuckle to smother the gateposts, ramblers to scramble
up trees, wallflowers, geraniums and lavender; all the
summer was to come. I climbed the hill and looked
down on the garden, sparkling in a green bowl with its
cluster of stone buildings surrounded by trees and water.
It was time to prepare a welcome for the family again –
the Easter holidays.

Chapter 12
APRIL

Of other gardens, co-operation or control; Eden and
THE LAP

'Keep me a place in this old land,
somewhere to grow, somewhere to be.'

From 'A Green Prayer' – written for children

This is not a book of learning, but a book about
learning. There are no lists of plants or diagrams
of herbaceous borders because everyone likes different kinds of flowers and I find it difficult to remember
all their names. But I have become familiar with some
of their characters and habits and have developed favourites. I love the strong scented things that intoxicate
on warm evenings after rain – honeysuckle, stocks and
broom, or lavender and rosemary to pinch as you walk
by; purple pansies and *Violas* – cheeky, smiling faces
peeping between rocks and dark red ones in the window box to match the velvet curtains; primroses and all

their relations, flowering year after year; daisies, big and small, from the tiny wild ones peppering the lawn to copper coloured chrysanthemums glowing through autumn afternoons; daffodils, bluebells, snowdrops and crocuses in ever increasing drifts among rough grass and trees, returning unattended; wisteria and clematis, climbing freely over anything that will support them. And roses; I have been falling in love with roses.

A friend who has a garden only yards from the sea, protected by willow and eucalyptus trees, has planted idyllic arbors of old fashioned, fragrant roses. They scramble up trees, arch over paths and peep from every corner. As we wander through the garden she introduces them all by name as if they were favourite nephews and nieces, including their lineage and individual qualities. I am leaning to love roses like that.

My parents were great gardeners, as were their parents, so I must have absorbed some things by osmosis. I have always had a garden, usually too big, and worked it myself not always with the joy this garden gives me now. There were times when gardening was, like housework, a chore that had to be fitted in on the run, a slash and burn activity, an attempt to control an overwhelming process rather than a creative relationship with growing things. When the work expands beyond capability, or inclination, it is time to make changes. In April I have to face the cutting of the grass and I will probably end up planning to reduce the lawn in favour of more bare rock and ground cover. Mowers, in my experience, are designed by men for men, without women in mind, except those who appear in the advertisements floating round something that looks like a green striped table cloth, with a cool complexion, perfect hair-do and immaculate

beach wear. Unfortunately the reality is full of contrasts. I drag out the monster, which is quite heavy and hard to disentangle from bicycles, wheelbarrow and beach toys, and begin to pull the string. I wear gloves because I know from experience that long before the thing explodes into life I shall have a raw blister between the two fingers that grip the string. I am stronger in the arms and shoulders than many women I know, even so for this job it is necessary to kick the machine forward with one leg while pulling backwards with the arm in order to spread the load and protect the lower back and stomach. I am sure it should be possible to invent something easier; we have been to the moon and back and we have circumnavigated Venus, yet technology is quite inadequate in this every day area. However, there are a few things that may help. The first is to get the thing serviced during the winter and empty the petrol out when you put it away at the end of the season. Then, having filled up with fresh petrol (of the correct mix – old mowers spurn the leadless kind) I unscrew the air filter and pour petrol through the carburettor before even trying to pull the string, to sluice out any foreign bodies that may have lodged there and to prime the system. After several fruitless efforts I may unscrew and wipe the inside of the sparking plug or warm it up a bit on the Aga – it should not be black with soot. If the engine starts and then stops I give the whole machine a good shake – lift it up and thump it down on the lawn. It may respond and it does me good. Finally, if everything fails, leave it to sulk; it may be too hot, too cold, too wet, tired or cross, as I am and a spell away from each other may do us both good. When I return, in a more relaxed frame of mind, it will probably have decided to co-operate. Or a new machine may be the answer. All these struggles did diminish when eventually that became possible. An even better solution would be to get someone else to do it.

The next thing about grass cutting is to attempt it only when the grass is dry. Nothing clogs the brute up more thoroughly than slabs of wet vegetation. Empty the box often, otherwise cuttings are spewed out all over the lawn and have to be raked up again. I dump lawn mowings all over the garden, as mulch under shrubs, roses and trees close to the lawn or put it all in the wheelbarrow and take it to the compost heap where a layer or two will rot down well between newspaper with dead ducklings and anything from the kitchen that might otherwise smell a bit. If you leave grass cuttings on a well populated lawn you will find they all end up inside the house, coming in on the rug you sunbathe on or everybody's shoes.

Long grass is a different matter. To encourage wild flowers it should not be cut until July. I cut paths through it with a strimmer because pushing a mower uphill in hot weather is exhausting. Strimming is noisy but quite satisfying because, instead of marching up and down, it entails weaving around things into corners and under shrubs and trees and along the edges of walls and boulders, which is fun, except that after an hour the arm bones and fingers vibrate in unison. It is advisable to wear wellies and goggles, or sunglasses, in case hard objects fly up at you, and remember that pale clothing may remain green for ever. In dry weather the long grass can be turned into hay and stored for poultry bedding.

Weeds come fast in April. They vary from place to place and from year to year. Some gardeners never seem to have them; the professionals rarely mention them. I have them all the time, from the dreaded knotweed that grows rock like roots four feet deep and sends up suckers yards away, to the insidious ground elder, bind weed and buttercup. Do not give way to any of these perennial invaders; even the buttercup, which looks so pretty in the wild, is a killer in the garden, swamping everything with a tenacious tangle of underground growth. My father invented a useful little tool for dealing with dandelions – a metal tube with a V cut out of one side, sharpened like a razor – which he plunged under each weed to cut the root low down. Sadly the stones in this garden soon blunten anything. I settle down, kneeling on a bit of carpet, with the hand pick, a sharp knife or a plasterers trowel and the radio. A bucket is rarely big enough – the best container is a builders' bag which contains as much as can be dragged to the bonfire or compost heap and easier than struggling up hill with a wheelbarrow. They come out much easier just after rain. Nettles come out better in dry weather while they are young, their surface roots loosened with a fork and yanked out in straggling mats. Brambles have thrived here for hundreds of years so it is a continuous, long term project getting rid of them. I have learned it is no use merely cutting them back, they have to be uprooted, but if you cut the roots just below the big knot where they begin, it does the trick. The growth above ground must be cut too or it re-roots wherever it touches the soil, and increases by yards in all directions every year, so I never find them all. Blackberries are better harvested from other people's hedgerows. Ground elder I pounce on wherever I see those nasty little wriggly white roots and I discovered, by accident, if you pile enough earth on top of the leaves it eventually dies of suffocation. This is also true of couch grass, so old carpets can be a help. Bracken has to be slashed three times a year for three years before it gives up. With annual weeds it is important to prevent them seeding, by pulling them out of cutting them down in time. I learned the hard way that farm manure, which has not been rotted down for a year or two, carries masses of hearty grass seeds to ruin all the hard work put into the vegetable plots. Old carpet, laid on top of compost at the end of the season is a wonderful labour saving trick. When you take it off in the spring the worms have done the digging for you and the soil is loose and ready for seeds, as long as you have not walked on it.

Weeds are simply plants we do not want, usually because they are so vigorous they threaten everything else. However, some so called weeds are very pretty. I encourage foxgloves; they move round the garden like an army, colonizing different places every year; herb robert, pennywort, ferns, milkwort, violets – I keep finding new wild flowers, which seed themselves. The Welsh poppy, yellow and orange, and rogue harlequins find their own places to grow and, this year, I gave up the battle with dandelions so parts of the yard were aglow with baby suns. I decided not to use weedkillers on the gravel so camomile and wild geraniums have moved in too. In other gardens the ground elder and nettles I treated with hormone weed killer and other poisonous potions, only returned and grew stronger, so here I am trying less destructive methods. I hate to see those areas of brown decimation where weed killers have been used. All too often precious plants are destroyed by mistake, as well as the habitat for useful bugs, beetles and butterflies.

Gardening friends are a great source of inspiration, information, plants and cuttings. One grows all sorts of rare things from seed and generously fills boxes with anonymous seedlings which take me by surprise as they mature into exotic creatures. Every garden is an expression of the personality of its maker. Hers is a forest of delicate specimens, grown from seeds collected from all over the world, sprouting in a jungle of greenhouses and conservatories and protected from westerly gales from the sea by wind bent evergreens. She has green fingers and prodigious botanical knowledge. Recently a new gazebo appeared, steps, a bird garden and a pond for her grandchildren who will soon be big enough to discover this paradise for themselves.

There is a garden across the valley which looks like a Persian carpet, with ever spreading clumps of flowers running into each other like a water colour painting. It was laid out on a slope, against a backdrop of hills, so perspective hardly exists. From the house it seems that the carpet is taking off into the sky.

Another garden on the same mountainside, has been carved out, with mechanical equipment, into a series of paved terraces, with stone steps, walls and even a stone bridge over a gushing stream. There are pots and pergolas and masses of expensive new shrubs. Although it faces north it feels like the Mediterranean, with sheltered places to sit in the sun when it climbs over the hill, all designed for minimum maintenance.

One town garden I know, a tiny fenced patch, takes on a new character each year as its owners adjust to their changing needs, abilities and interests. At first the soil was built up on top of natural sand and gravel until it was producing prize wining vegetables – giant leeks, onions, beans, marrows and tomatoes. Paths were edged with miniature cordons of apples and pears, roses and sweet peas – everything won prizes. Later it was re-planned for a more leisurely life, with places to sit, hanging baskets overflowing with flowers and a specially landscaped environment for miniature ducks, with a miniature duck house and a miniature pond. Every year new things happen there, a new deep bed at waist height for lettuces and herbs, a bigger green house for more tomatoes, an extension for budgerigars, a fishpond – what goes into this garden is as inspiring as what comes out.

My daughter has created gorgeous jungles on the flat roofs and balconies of city flats. A couple of animal lovers have made a flowering sanctuary for birds, butterflies, dogs and decorative ducks. My grandson made a pond to attract newts with a house for a gheko. Another grandmother's garden began as a labour of love in memory of her husband and grew into an expression of her own way of living, a seasonal ritual of gentle care and attention which produces quantities of fruit for jam making, asparagus, tomatoes, salad and grapes for the table. It is a setting for birds that feed outside the window, for badgers that dance under the pines in the moonlight, for friends who wander round a gracefully ordered wilderness. In fact the organization includes some clever tricks like mulching fruit bushes with newspaper, pouring a boiling kettle on the paths while the weeds are young and the setting of plants to give maximum effect with minimum attention. A huge camelia frames the view of the mountains, drifts of crimson primulas fill the boggy places, cyclamen thrive under pine trees. You walk from one contained space to another, each with a different mood and aspect; old roses line the path to the vegetable plots, raised with stout planks between pebble paths, built up every year with compost, walls support cherries and pears. I am inspired by what is possible.

She appears in a garden apron with huge pockets, cool as a cucumber, without a hair awry – a brown – skinned pixie lady, utterly at home in a world of rhythms, reasons and seasons, in no need to hurry.

Nearby is yet another kind of garden which reassures me because maintenance is never done.

This has become a totally wild place where birds and small animals thrive undisturbed in layers of vegetation like a rain forest, all intertwined with convolvulus. A winding path is cleared through it, that is all. When I can no longer manage the mower and am too stiff to do the weeding, I could let most of this garden revert to nature like that, cut a way through to seats and views and sit a listen to birdsong and the sound of water. By then all the trees will be huge, roses, clematis and honeysuckle will have their way with them and there should still be masses of flowering bulbs pushing through to the light each spring.

Taking part in this process of growth, and its pauses, can spread its effect beyond the garden or the back yard. We may learn to respect nature and treat it with reverence. Time spent in a garden is well spent. If it becomes a chore, it might be best to pave it over and plant a few pots with *Pelargoniums*. If the making and tending of a garden is life enhancing, the garden will be.

* * *

The garden of Eden is a universal metaphor for the growth of our species, the setting for the beginning of evolution of the human race on earth. Adam and Eve symbolize the male and female principles of the human psyche. Between them they made a choice, as we all do every day, between acting from awareness or from fear; with trust, wisdom and compassion or with doubt, anger or shame. We can create paradise, or be cast out; we can create with love and respect or with pride and ambition. The serpent – the creature that moves so close to the earth, changes its skin and eats its own tail – is temptation, but it also offers an opportunity to pause and consider the results of our behaviour before we act, a chance to look and listen, to change the situation – to heal. Evil is live spelled backwards – every word is a kind of spell.

Lucifer is also the light bringer. Adam and Eve symbolize two kinds of energy, two sides of our nature, so, if we can connect compassionately to both parts of ourselves we can connect more compassionately with others and live in peace.

The Tree of Knowledge is to do with the power of naming, or owning. We think, once we have given a name to something we have, as it were, taken it over, boxed it in. The greatest experience to be had from nature is not to do with naming at all, but with being part of it. This can be frightening because we are small and fragile faced with ocean waves, mountain screes, wind and tide. However, we can share this energy if we let it carry us along. When John Fowles writes – 'Art and nature are siblings, branches of the one tree; and nowhere more than in the continuing inexplicabilities of many of their processes...' he is affirming a mistrust of ever increasing information, which is the apple from the Tree of Knowledge that separates us from paradise. When I smell a rose the scent is not increased because I know its name, although I do also need to know how to ask for it.

* * *

When new neighbours came to inhabit the empty mill barn next door and immediately hacked most of the branches off the beautiful sycamore tree that had been part of the view for five years, I was sad and angry. When a JCB started to move a lot of rock and drowned all other sounds I realised how territorial I was becoming about my little patch of Eden. Money could reduce this piece of Welsh mountainside to suburban real estate in no time and there was nothing I could do about it. When the mill pond was suddenly drained, because it was considered hazardous, I had to move the geese and dig a new goose pond. I inspected my territory and discovered that, after a wet winter, new springs were dribbling into a declivity behind the pig sties. Nearby was a great heap of broken slate and rubble that had been dumped there when the barn was re-roofed. After clearing the low ground of brambles I realised I could make a dam between two huge stone gateposts with a stout sheet of corrugated iron and that rubble. Once again it was the trenching tool that did it; rake and spade gave me back ache. At the end of each day clothes and hair were plastered with mud but, as the hole grew deeper, the dam grew higher. It was very satisfying and helped to purge my anger about the mutilated tree, the dead fish and the loss of all those lovely reflections of hills and sky, with a floating sun or moon, once visible from the footpath. The goslings hatched and were shepherded into their new home just before the JCB demolished their old one. It was some comfort to watch them swimming on the new pond.

Easter had come with such terrible weather that, although we did collect some white stones from the beach for the maze, the gravel was still in a pile in the yard. Little by little, in half barrow loads, I struggled uphill to spread it, while next door the pneumatic drills, diggers and earth moving monsters roared and rumbled for months. There was even talk of dynamite to shift the bedrock. I remembered the old gardener who seemed to spend so much of his time leaning on his spade watching robins, now I understood – one barrow load, then a bit of pruning; another and a cup of tea. It took a week to dig the new pond and spread the gravel on the maze. I decided to wait for the children to help me lay the white stones.

I was trimming the hole in the hedge, made so we could see the sea from the kitchen, when it occurred to me that a hedge with a series of arches in it could be useful in suburban gardens. An arched hedge still gives shelter because the wind flows over it, but it casts less shade. It could be a compromise, where priorities differ, between shade, sunshine and shelter, privacy and a view. After a sleepless night at full moon, part of which I spent sitting by the spring struggling with my territorial instincts and wishing that the hazel tree would drop a few nuts of wisdom into the pool, I realised it was time to build The Lap – a secret seat hidden at the heart of my garden, where I could sit and discover the internal space that is the powerhouse of miracles, while the space around me was so painfully under threat.

* * *

Our prehistoric ancestors moved masses of earth and

stone, shaping the land for mysterious purposes. They also diverted water and lopped trees. We shall never know exactly what they were doing, any more than future generations will know what we were up to, in spite of all our records. We see the past through our personal view finders. If an archeologist came upon The Lap, no doubt he would presume it was a throne – that is how we look at history. Cadair Idris is the chair, or throne of the giant Idris, from which he was able to study the stars. This seat will be a green lady inviting you to sit in her lap and discover that the present is the only place to be.

I began by making sketches and then models with clay from the pond. I remembered the way children had clambered all over the huge bronze figures by Henry Moore. They invited physical contact. When the sculptor was asked if he minded these attentions and he replied that, since trainers had replaced hob nailed boots, there was no problem, this had reassured members of the Salisbury Planning Authority when the Arts Centre, in the redundant church of St Edmund, were able to borrow a reclining lady and display it in the churchyard for a few years. Children always curled up in her lap.

There was an old arm chair in the barn, too big for the house, with a solid wooden frame; I wrapped it in a sheet of thick polythene, from someone's swimming pool, to protect it from damp and insects; added wooden shoulders, a log of wood for the neck and an old climbing helmet for the head. The body was covered with odd bits of chicken wire and rubble was piled round it like a skirt. I consulted a book on sculpture, mixed cement with lime and red sand, which dried to a nice flesh tone, and plastered layers all over this framework. Each layer was allowed to dry for a few days and covered in case it rained. A few smooth stones were added as knees and shoulders to give the impression of solid rock, or stone bones. The elbows were planted with thyme, the head with trailing periwinkle and ivy. An old lampshade frame strengthened the head and gave honeysuckle something to climb through, like hair. Once again serendipity worked; I wandered round my accumulation of junk for ideas until things presented themselves. The lampshade kept asking to be used but I could not see how until, one day, I balanced it on top of the helmet – and there was the head with a halo and support for the neck and hair. When The Lap was finished it settled down well against the dark background of evergreens. The ash trees round the quartz maze at her feet threw their moving shadows over her and I planted red and white tulips in the long grass on either side to symbolize the sun and moon. To sit here on a moonlit summer night and listen to the rustle of leaves and the sound of the stream is to enter another world. The Greek word *Temenos* means a sacred space outside the temple, but this temple is not man made. Anyone who sits here is reminded of that. There is a time capsule hidden in the statue to tell its story.

As an aging gardener now
allow the seasons to invent your days.
Rampaging out of April
energy returns like sap to move the earth
and make new mountains out of molehills.

This lap is not a throne,
but set in secret where a maze unwinds,
was made to seat a soul.

The last day of April.

I have been walking in the early morning garden; the sun is just rising and brightening a few patches of golden rushes along the river bank, just touching the standing stone. The cockerel is crowing and one duck, returning from a night out, woke me by quacking loudly for its mate. A mist is rolling in from the sea shining and shifting as it creeps by like pink candy floss. One night last week, unable to sleep, I sat under the willow and watched the full moon shiver in the pool; now half of it hangs in a pale blue sky; the ceanothus is bright blue, violets a mauve mist under the rocks, daffodils tall in the hedge. Yesterday was the first day I felt the air was green again, heavy with sap and juices. The cuckoo, calling from the wood for the first time, went on calling for five minutes. And the swallows are back, darting under the eaves, searching for last years nests.

POSTSCRIPT

'The spaces of the world full circle
turn
Into the nought where all began.'

'The Hollow Hill' – Kathleen Raine.

*Now it is May again, the magic month. Twelve
have passed and the moon is full again. Clematis
foams further over the wall and along the pergola,
swallows swoop and dive through the sunshine, vegetables are growing green; visitors arrive and gasp
with delight, follow paths and sit on seats. The days
grow long, the evenings light. I sit outside to write.
I want to slow down the process, relish it a little
longer. This happens every year.*

A garden is a sanctuary, something we recreate
out of something we lost, perhaps, a memory of
childhood or innocence, an individual Eden. A year ago,
walking in the garden by night, I wrote 'I am frightened
that the spell may break.' Now I know it is unbreakable

as long as it never becomes static and fragile like ice, but flows like water. Working in the garden is one way of ensuring 'There is no end to the procession of present moments.'

One year on a new generation of ducks are swimming in the pond; the ceanothus survived a terrible winter; a new rose is replacing the tree lupin; rhododendrons, planted for shelter, are in flower for he first time and will soon become an impenetrable screen between the garden and its approaches. Land and air are alive with 'all the greens, like a family of snaky essences' as Edward Thomas put it. Every evening I am overpowered by the intoxicating scent of honeysuckle and stocks. Tonight I may walk in the garden again under a new moon. The April moon was the twelfth one and it gave me a sleepless night of transformation and completion. Next week the garden will be populated by children again, finding paths and making new ones. As Richard Maybe wrote in his Home Country – 'To children landscape is less a matter of looking than touching and using... perhaps making. We grow through a whole gamut of responses – an animal sense of territory, a spell of animism, various Dark Age brands of magic and primitive science – before graduating to the sensible adult view of land as Real Estate...'

I know I never graduated.

I am lucky to be able to share my second childhood with my children sometimes and watch their children discover things for themselves. I hope they will make their own real and lasting connections strongly enough to withstand the tumults of technology that threaten the future and find a way through their own mazes. May this garden grow fertile memories.

Ty'r Gawen – May 1st 1996

AFTERWORD

The garden has grown, the trees are huge, the daffodils are coming out and the world has changed again. Information technology has transformed it. As I prepare this book for a wider public, I realise that it might seem out of date. But I still hope that its message is appropriate and useful and may inspire others to follow their dreams, whatever they may be.

Ty'r Gawen – March 2012

15244628R00107

Printed in Great Britain
by Amazon.co.uk, Ltd.,
Marston Gate.